"Alan Guebert is the rare writer who eloquently combines his personal story and journey with where agriculture is headed. With humor and honesty Guebert tells like it is—and gives his readers the tools to fight for a food and agriculture system that is fair for farmers and workers and safe and healthy for eaters. I recommend this book to anyone who wants to hear the story of food from someone who has been following it for the last three decades."
—DANIELLE NIERENBERG, President, Food Tank

"A wonderful piece of work. It's authentic and highly descriptive without being smothered in adjectives. It's also personal and reflective without being overly sentimental. A celebration of a life well lived even if some day-to-day aspects of that life were challenging and exhausting."
—FRED MYERS, winner, Lifetime Achievement Award from the American Agriculture Editors' Association

"Alan is a rare gift to farmers and non-farmers alike since he provides down-home wisdom that helps us all make sense of the important, but often misunderstood food and farm issues. *The Land of Milk and Uncle Honey* is a treasure—the best of the best."
—FRED KIRSCHENMANN, author of *Cultivating an Ecological Conscience*

THE LAND OF MILK
OF MILK
AND UNCLE HONEY

THE LAND OF MILK AND UNCLE HONEY

MEMORIES FROM THE FARM OF MY YOUTH

ALAN GUEBERT

WITH
MARY GRACE FOXWELL

UNIVERSITY OF ILLINOIS PRESS
URBANA, CHICAGO, AND SPRINGFIELD

Library of Congress Cataloging-in-Publication Data
Guebert, Alan, author.
The land of milk and Uncle Honey : memories from the farm
of my youth / Alan Guebert ; with Mary Grace Foxwell.
pages cm
ISBN 978-0-252-08094-4 (pbk. : alk. paper) —
ISBN 978-0-252-09748-5 (e-book)
1. Guebert, Alan.
2. Dairy farmers—Illinois—Biography.
3. Dairy farming—Illinois—Anecdotes.
I. Foxwell, Mary Grace, author. II. Title.
SF229.7.G83G84   2015
636.2'14209773—dc23   2014042887

To all the Uncle Honeys, Jackies, and Howards now long gone in a forever-gone era of hired men, dinner at noon, and plain, honest work. What they gave us didn't cost a nickel; how they gave it to us was priceless.

And to the lovely Catherine, I am because you are.

CONTENTS

ACKNOWLEDGMENTS

No one person stands alone in any achievement. Even the sailor who crosses the Pacific solo owes due thanks to the builder of his seaworthy craft, the cartographer of necessary charts, and the old salt who, literally, showed him the ropes. The same is true of this voyage, spanning more than thirty years of solo freelance writing and weekly column writing. There are many to acknowledge and thank.

Two who stand at the front of the long line are Bob Hays and Theodore Peterson, both professors at the University of Illinois. Hays was a writer's editor from southern Illinois. He was quiet, strong, and caring. Peterson was an editor's editor who stapled two dollars to my first story draft in his class and ordered me to the "Illini Union bookstore to buy Strunk and White's *The Elements of Style* and spend a night reading it." I did, and the worn, little book sits on my desk yet today.

My writing life would not have happened without Mary Louise Rea, an English professor, whose almost-motherly guidance greatly influenced my studies, my family, and my future. I hope her Great Reward is just as she dreamed: an eternal seminar with Thoreau, Melville, Dickenson, and Twain.

Once I landed in the field, many ensured that I took root. There was Mike Walsten, Bob Coffman, and Paul Wilcox at *Professional Farmers of America* and Rich Krumme, Larry Reichenberger, Greg Wood, and Danita Allen Wood at *Successful Farming* magazine.

And there was Robin Hoffman, Reichenberger's former associate editor, whose departure from *Successful Farming* for *Farm Journal* created the opening I filled. When I chose to go the full-time freelance route in 1984, Robin, then editor of *Top Producer*, bought every word of every story I wrote for nearly a decade.

And he bought every one unwritten and unread. Robin was the only editor I've ever had who was that trusting, that generous.

I never would have had those great teachers and editors had my parents, Richard and Twila Guebert, not given me the foundation from which to climb toward those seemingly unreachable stars. They encouraged me to read, learn, and try.

My biggest believers, however, were John and Kitty Watson, my father- and mother-in-law, who not once doubted my career choices despite the dozen or so chances I gave them. That's true encouragement; that's love.

Much inspiration and encouragement also came from several literary and professional giants. A very short list of these very kind, very complimentary people includes Wendell Berry, Gene Logsdon, Fred Kirschenmann, Charlie Sing, C. Robert Taylor, Phil St John, James Lieber, and David Hoech.

Writers, of course, need readers, and the readers of the Farm and Food File are some of the most loyal, engaged readers in journalism—not an easy thing for today's shrinking farm and newspaper fields. Thank you for your time each week over these decades to share ideas, opinions, and memories. The conversation has been, and continues to be, grand.

This book is also the result of the great talent and very hard work of daughter Mary Grace Foxwell. While the idea of writing these columns may have been mine, compiling them into a heartfelt collection was all Gracie's. She pulled and pushed it—and me—from start to finish, editing every word, sentence, and paragraph. The best sign of an excellent editor is the editor leaves no fingerprints. That's Gracie. When I review her edits, I think only one thing: wow, I'm good. Truth is, I'm not. My editor, however, is.

Gracie also brings to this project an extensive network of talented, creative friends whose respect and love for each other carries through in all mutual efforts. One of those efforts now rests in your hands: this book's cover design by Daphne Karagianis. Gracie and Daphne met in the fourth grade; an instant later, Daphne was, and remains, a daughter. Gracie is words; Daphne is art. This book is a twin testament to what these two, talented sisters-of-the-heart mean to the lovely Catherine and me.

Most importantly, none of these events and nothing in my career would have happened without Catherine. Longtime column readers know her as "the lovely Catherine"; I know her as my life force because my life changed the second I saw her cross the street outside my Newman Hall dormitory window in Champaign, IL, in 1974. Forty years later, she remains just as lovely and I remain the luckiest farmboy ever.

These columns acknowledge an all-but-forgotten time in American agriculture. Each is a snapshot of life and the many lives on a bustling, 1960s dairy farm in southern Illinois. Sincere thanks is owed to a fellow farmboy, Michael Roux, and his colleagues at the University of Illinois Press for beautifully preserving that life, and those who lived it, for future generations. Their honest, unexceptional lives should be remembered.

Now they will.

PROLOGUE

The Farm and Food File began one drizzly winter night almost forty-five years ago when, elbow-deep into pulling wet-as-rags corn stalks out of a five-bottom plow, I looked into the low, starless sky and muttered to myself, "There's got to be something better than this."

What that might be I hadn't a clue—which, also, was why I was attempting to plow mud that night in 1978. A year before, I had confessed to a dean at the University of Illinois that I didn't have a lot of motivation to complete my degree. I think I said something as thoughtfully prepared as "Uh, I don't know if I want to be here anymore."

The dean, a caring and inspiring man named Warren Wessels, looked across his cluttered desk, lit his pipe, and rose from his chair.

"Excuse me for a moment," he said as he walked out the door of his small office.

He returned a couple of minutes later with a contrail of pipe smoke in his wake, and slid back into his chair. "Well," he said with a hint of breathlessness, "that's done."

"Done? What's done?"

"You are," he replied calmly. "You said that you didn't know if you wanted to be here. Fine, I know people who do. So, as of two minutes ago, you are no longer a student and they are. You're out."

Dean Wessels drew a few deep breaths to re-kindle his pipe as he watched the blood drain from my face. He allowed a long silent moment to pass so the full effect of his action was felt.

"By the way," he said finally, "when you want back in—and you will—come and see me and I'll do everything I can to help." He then stood up and extended his arm to shake my hand. I cautiously did the same, and left.

And, just like that, I was out of the Big U. Cashiered not by Dean Wessels but by my indecision, my laziness, and my mouth.

So home to southern Illinois I went. Home to my father as my full-time boss. Home to the seemingly endless acres where I had grown up, with its 100-cow dairy, handful of hired men, my older brother (a recent ag college graduate) and all its hay baling, manure hauling, cow milking, corn planting, soybean cultivation, and fall plowing.

It was the only home I had ever known. Now, though, it wasn't so much a home as a sanctuary; a place to live, work, and wonder what I was really going to do with my life. Was I to be a dairy farmer like my father or something else? What else? The only thing certain in my life then was the lovely Catherine, my spouse of less than a year. I was not certain, however, that she wanted to be the wife of a dairy farmer.

But home to the southern Illinois dairy farm of my youth we went.

The farm, located a good walk from where the-then slow, meandering Kaskaskia River flowed into the roiling Mississippi, was named Indian Farm in recognition of the region's rich Native American heritage. The wide, flat river bottoms—a tiny section of the lengthy, Mississippi-dominated area that old American maps often labeled the "Great American Bottoms"—had been the home village of the Kaskaskia Indians and their leader, Chief Du Quoin.

The Kaskaskias were peaceful people, accepting the pioneer settlers who came up the Mississippi to establish Illinois in their front yard. Kaskaskia, a French trading village five miles downstream from Indian Farm, was the seat of British colonial influence in the region and, in 1818, became Illinois' first capital. In 1881, the Mississippi claimed the channel of the nearby Kaskaskia River as well as the city of the same name that sat on its muddy banks.

The story of my family's time on that land is different than the usual American family farm narrative, however. We didn't homestead it, didn't build it over generations, didn't reclaim it from nature. My grandfather Victor Guebert, a St. Louis stockbroker by trade, pieced it together in the mid-1940s simply as an investment for clients and himself. One client and farm partner was his younger brother, Lorenz, a nearby town's milk deliveryman. (Lorenz was my great-uncle's given name; Honey was his aptly given nickname.) Two other partners were non-farming businessmen who Grandpa advised on all things cash and coin.

Our farmstead looking northeast, bordered by the Kaskaskia River and the rolling hills of southern Illinois. Trees conceal the farmhouse; Indian Farm's dairy, silos, and hay barns are farther south down Lock and Dam Road, just out of view.

Indian Farm was unique in other ways, too.

First, it had been surveyed and platted by the French, so each parcel of land, no matter its geographic relation to the Mississippi, came with a deeded pathway to the river. Locals called these paths "granny strips" because, inversely, they remained "grandfathered" in as the land was sold and resold. While they stretched miles long, they were no more than ten yards wide. (My father often joked that he'd take "breakfast, dinner, and supper" with him when he'd farm the granny strips because a round trip to and from the river could take more than an hour.)

Another unique aspect of Indian Farm was the bold plan my non-farming grandfather held for it: a 100-cow, Grade A dairy to maximize both the land and the labor of the more than 700-acre operation. It was an audacious plan for someone who hadn't put his shoulder into the flank of a milk cow since American doughboys were fighting the Hun in France.

My grandfather Victor Guebert (far left) and Uncle Honey (far right), photographed with their siblings in 1946. Formally, left to right: Victor, Walter, Carl, Norma, Arnold, Alfred, and Lorenz. Informally: Grandpa, Walks, Chunky, Little Norm, Dick, Bank, and Honey. Aunt Norma, who gave me the photo in the early 1990s, remembered that day well. She said Grandpa, a stockbroker in St. Louis, wore more fashionable, summertime trousers while his brothers wore more conservative, dark attire. His brothers teased my grandfather over his "dandy" appearance (note the cane) and he promised to never wear light-colored trousers again. Norma and I agreed; he never did.

Two other factors made Indian Farm especially interesting. When Grandpa Guebert, Uncle Honey, and the two others bought the land parcel-by-parcel, they also acquired the tenants parcel-by-parcel. Many of the tenant farmers moved on to other nearby farms, a common practice in that common occupation of the 1940s. One family of four brothers and their mother, however, stayed. Three of the four brothers would eventually work on Indian Farm for some, or all, of the next four decades.

One brother, Jackie, the subject of several columns, worked 6:00 a.m. to 6:00 p.m., six days a week, fifty-one weeks a year for many decades as the farm's principal field hand, tractor driver, and hypochondriac. My return to the farm in 1978, I am embarrassed to report, ended his longstanding tenure; I replaced Jackie. My father, I still suspect, wonders if it was a good exchange.

Another brother, Howard, worked even longer days, usually 4:30 a.m. until 7:00 p.m., as the farm's 100 percent reliable, 100 percent caring, dairy herdsman. Howard had an even pace that carried him through both the dairy barn and life with few stumbles. He wasn't fast and he wasn't slow, and he smiled more than he laughed. He also would take a couple of hours off every afternoon to lounge or nap—no one ever gave him a schedule and no one ever tracked his time—to make it through his long, long days, year after year after year.

Howard was special because he was so un-special. He was the most honest, calm, and loyal person I've ever met. We often shared cow-milking chores on weekends because the double-six herringbone parlor required two full-time milkers to operate at capacity. Before long I was calling him "Hoard the Dairy-man" after the well-known dairy magazine of the era, *Hoard's Dairyman*, and he called me "Allie Boy" from the first day we met when I was, truly, just a boy.

The other, quite interesting aspect of Indian Farm was its decades-long, day-to-day manager: my father. Dad grew up in "town," the only son of the gifted "numbers guy," my grandfather the stockbroker. Grandpa, however, had grown up on a farm, no more than eight city blocks from where he was raising his family. That meant Dad would often walk to the farm as a young boy, which by then was operated by Grandpa's brother, Uncle Bank, to piddle, fiddle, and learn farming.

It must have taken because, after World War II, Dad cashed in his GI Bill benefits at the University of Illinois' College of Agriculture. Afterwards, he and my mother bought a small, hilly farm to operate once they married in 1950. Uncle Sam had other plans, however, and after almost a year of reserve Army duty north of Chicago, they finally returned to their chickens, lambs, pigs, cows, draft horses, and crops.

Not for long, however. By 1954, Mom and Dad were installed on Indian Farm as its boss pair. I don't know the whole story—it's still a sore subject with my mother—on how it came about for them to sell their little piece of American agriculture to operate, but not own, Grandpa and his pals' really big piece of pasture, corn, and cows.

By the time I arrived in June 1955, my parents were running the farm and its several hundred acres, a massive dairy, a half-dozen hired men, and, in just few months short of five years of marriage, four children. (Just a few years later, there'd be six children.) Dad was 28, Mom 23.

How did they do it?

I don't know, but a key part of it, I suspect, was just doing it; getting up every morning and just moving forward with life and work and family. There was,

My mother, Twila, holding me in the living room of her parents' home, Thanksgiving 1955. Indeed, I was already looking like a holiday turkey.

of course, far more to do than whatever would, or could, get done in a day, so staying busy wasn't a problem.

Moreover, my people are German Lutheran. Let me rephrase that; my people are heads-down, nose-to-the-wheel German Lutheran. Work was (is) a big part of life and life was (is) a gift from God. As such, work was (is) part of God's good plan for you and your happiness.

Does that make sense? Well, it would if you were raised German Lutheran on a southern Illinois dairy farm.

All that work meant that my brothers, sister, and I would become important parts of Indian Farm. In our early youth, we helped our mother in the kitchen, around the house, and in the huge acre-and-a-half garden. We cleaned, canned, and complained every day of our young childhood.

But we also ate southern Illinois peaches in January that tasted like July, and lathered homemade bread with apple butter whose smell took you right back to the giant, stir-stir-stir copper kettle in the backyard last August. We cleaned carp, grew turnips, and planted enough sweet potatoes that we could share 'em with the groundhogs that then waddled into winter.

When we finally got tall enough in years and legs, around the real-work-ready age of ten or eleven, my father would recruit us to drive a small tractor to rake hay, or slowly guide a tractor and wagon through a hayfield on humid summer mornings so a crew of hard-muscled hired men could pick up and stack the bales from my father's late work the evening before.

It was both exhausting and exhilarating, working with the tough-as-leather hired men who taught us stable boys how to cuss. That made us men, right? Well, at least we weren't canning green beans anymore.

Fieldwork brought another benefit over housework: pay. My father was the rare farmer who paid his children for their help on the farm. His standing rate (for a decade with me) was fifty cents per hour. No, it wasn't much; but it was fifty times more than neighbor boys were earning and, moreover, he allowed us to keep track of our own hours.

On the fifteenth and last day of every month, my father asked us for our "hours" and Mom would simply write us a paycheck. We knew that a fat share of those earnings had to be saved for post–high school education. What or where that was to be was not specifically discussed or even planned; bi-monthly trips to our local bank, however, were.

My mother made it quite plain and quite early that my university choices should include her top two picks: the University of Illinois, Dad's alma mater, or Concordia Seminary, her brother's alma mater. So it was to be ag something or another, or the Lutheran ministry. It might not have been much of a choice but it was a pretty clear choice.

In mid-August 1973, my father and mother drove me and a footlocker of almost all my material possessions to 604 E. Armory Street in Champaign, IL. That was, and remains, the address of Newman Hall. Naturally, I had landed at the Roman Catholic dormitory in the heart of campus. The 200-mile trek to Newman Hall that blisteringly hot Sunday brought two personal firsts: it was the farthest from home I had ever been in my life, and it was the farthest north I had ever been in my life. I felt worlds away from Randolph County and couldn't wait to soak it all in.

And so, after three years of soaking "it" in and patronizing every watering hole on and off campus, I ended up in the smoke-clouded office of Dean Wessels. The ag something or another thing wasn't sorting itself out and he cleverly thought a return trip to the other side of the academic fence, Indian Farm, might hold the cure.

The farmlot and flat fields looking north from our farmhouse. Spring, mid-1960s. The field directly behind the plow is where, as a boy, I discovered many Native American artifacts. It's also where, on a dishrag-wet spring night in 1978, a muddy session with that plow led me from the well-known Indian Farm into the unknown.

More than a year after my departing handshake, I was still on the farm and still looking for a cure, or at least a sign of a cure.

That fall had been a wet and sloppy one. Little harvest fieldwork, mostly plowing, had gotten done. Winter was worse; a dripping blanket of gray skies and boot-sucking mud. When March sun finally broke through, the unfinished fall plowing became the yet-to-do spring plowing. And that meant the least senior farm employee, me, was parked on the plow and told not to get off until the entire farm had been turned.

I was told one more thing; if I finished plowing within ten days, I would earn a $100 bonus, nearly a half-month's pay.

So plowing I went. And went and went. Two times a day, usually at the sixes—6:00 a.m. and 6:00 p.m., I'd pour diesel into the big Ford and go, until it—and me—couldn't go anymore. In between, I'd hike down the road to the 50-ft. by 12-ft. trailer I shared with the lovely Catherine to grab a nap and a sandwich, and then I'd go at it again.

One long night and one short day shy of completing the job and grabbing the bonus, a gentle spring rain began to fall. Within an hour the drizzle caused the now-wet cornstalks to hang on the plow's big shanks and, as they did, they caught more stalks. Soon the plow was a mound of moving cornstalks instead of a farm implement. I stopped twice to unplug the muddy mess; the second time turned me into the muddy mess.

The third time was the last time. The stalks, the mud, the rain, my tired eyes, all combined to jam the plow with what seemed like a huge wall of failure. I dismounted the tractor and walked into the dark, drizzly night to take a measure. I couldn't clear it—the plow or the wall. That's when I looked upward into the starless darkness and moaned, "There's got to be something better, something else, than this." Something better or something else didn't have an exact meaning but it didn't have rain, cornstalks, or mud either—the next day, or the next decade. Something better was simply something different than plowing ten days straight at ten bucks a day—that day or 1,000 days into the future.

Tired and defeated, I climbed back on the Ford and steered the muddy, wet rig out of the slippery field and into the barn. Shortly thereafter I went to bed, a few hours short of finishing and what seemed like a nickel or two short of the $100 bonus. One of my grandfather's original partners paid me the $100 anyway. "You'd have earned it if it hadn't rained," he explained. "Besides, you're going to finish when it dries." He was right; I did.

A few days later, some daydreaming took me back to the Big U and the gatekeeper dean. If there was something better for me than plowing black, southern Illinois gumbo in the rain, the path to it must lay through him and that gate he held, I reckoned.

Three months later, a visit to Champaign brought Catherine and me to Mumford Hall, the College of Agriculture building at the Big U. While Catherine walked to some of our old campus haunts, I dropped by to visit what I hoped was a friend.

As I entered Dean Wessel's office, he rose and extended his hand, but before I could shake it he looked me squarely in the face and said, "Yes, if you're ready."

I almost cried. How did I merit so much confidence from a person I had so disappointed and hadn't so much as even telephoned in nearly two years?

It wasn't going to be an easy re-entry, he warned. "You'll be on an academic probation. And to make sure you come back ready to work," Wessels explained, "your probation will be B+. Anything short of that and you'll be gone again—and for good."

I was too happy to argue. All I needed to do was tell my parents that I was headed back to school and, secondly, figure out how I was going to get the best grades of my college life.

The first part was surprisingly easy; my parents encouraged my return to school.

The second problem had an equally evident solution: writing. If I needed to post some great grades, I had to take classes I knew I could sail through. That meant just one type of class, something with writing . . . journalism, English, communications, something . . .

Then serendipity struck. The College of Agriculture offered a few classes in an area labeled "Agricultural Communications" and, by pure chance, there was room for one more student in ag comm's basic "campaigns" class taught by a courtly editor from southern Illinois named Bob Hays.

Bob was one of those people that, from the second you meet, you know is going to be very important in your life. His handshake, shy smile, and two steady eyes conspired to make you relax, listen, and share. He was a wonderful teacher, a careful editor, an advisor, friend, and mentor; someone who would cut through the bureaucracy so one of his budding writers might flower.

From the beginning, Bob seemed to know me from a former life. He guided me through the B+ probation, encouraged me to take more journalism classes, found a few hundred dollars in scholarship money for me and Catherine, introduced me to visiting professionals, steered me to important books that would not be used in the classroom but were necessary for a more complete education and, most of all, became a great friend.

After receiving an A in Bob's class that first semester back on campus and successfully getting through my probation, the rest was easy.

Well, mostly. The good grades and the great fun in the classes that delivered them encouraged me to jump out of ag econ and into ag communications. The move meant another eighteen months of tuition, books, part-time jobs (short order cook, metal press operator, newspaper delivery boy, dormitory handyman, house painter, apartment building manager) and even more student loans.

Did I mention the birth of son Paul halfway through that first year back? The lovely Catherine had thankfully graduated with an education degree before my college hiatus, and she had been teaching throughout my navel-gazing years.

The return to academic rigor, unlike that dark, wet night plowing, was completely unscripted and wonderfully exciting. Every day brought new challenges, new ideas, new hope. And it all came along so beautifully that it could not have been just a lovely accident; someone was leading and this long-ago Lutheran schoolboy knows Who.

Paulie Boy and me in front of Mumford Hall at the University of Illinois. Spring 1980, a year after the lovely Catherine and I had returned to the Big U so I could complete my degree.

Through it all—developing black and white film after midnight, typing magazine stories in the basement so not to wake tiny Paul, eating hotdogs and sauerkraut three days a week, taking advantage of free movie nights at the Urbana library (free popcorn, too; we called that supper), being slipped a twenty-dollar bill by Catherine's father John in his departing handshake every time he and his always-believing-in-me spouse Kitty visited, eating sack lunches with the lovely Catherine and ever-happy Paulie Boy in the many hidden campus courtyards, and on and on—everything was better than pulling wet corn stalks from a muddy, five-bottom plow on a rainy, chilly night in March.

And none of it would have happened without that plow, that rain, that mud, that night, that farm. I left it long ago and, yes, there was something better for me after I did. But it was that farm, that beautiful piece of southern Illinois sand and gumbo, which made all of my writing, these stories, and my life possible. Its every acre remains in my marrow, its people in my heart.

I've been asked if I would do it all again—leaving farming and that land—given the choice today. In truth, nothing can replace the sights, sounds, and smells of a boyhood on a big farm and absolutely nothing can replace the people of

Graduation Day, May 1981. After seven years, you bet I wanted a picture to prove that the Big U had "happily" sent me into my future.

that farm and my youth. All played a part in making me me. But I didn't leave Indian Farm, or farming, because of the hard work it demanded. I loved the hard work because, at the end of the day, something important had been done and I and everyone else could see it. Nor did I leave it because something better awaited. I didn't know what awaited. Leaving was very much a gamble but a gamble Catherine and I agreed we'd take because we were young, adventurous, and willing to roll the dice once or twice.

I left because I simply had to. I had to go over that far hill I could see but didn't know what lay beyond. I would always want to know what was beyond, so I simply had to go without knowing if the lovely Catherine or I would return.

Ironically, or perhaps not, I wound up with a "farm" of my own: a national weekly column that investigates, reports, and explains the issues and people at the center of America's farm and food policies and politics. Sometimes that can be as hard and sweaty work as baling hay in August or combining wheat in June.

And, yet, when I want to leave the column, politics, and policies, I instinctively go back to that hill for a look at Indian Farm. There remains my youth, my family, the hired men, and the hard work that made my current work possible.

I don't miss it because I never left it and it never left me.

SPRING

PLANT

There was a peaceful, nearly silent ebb and flow to the seasons on Indian Farm. Spring rarely sprung on us because the mild winters in southern Illinois rarely locked us in. The days simply got longer, warmer, and more colorful as did the fieldwork and acres before us. All held the promise of a new year of better harvests, better profit, better times.

THE PATH TO HEAVEN
APRIL 4, 2010

Somewhere in my parents' home exists a photograph of them standing stiffly on either side of my oldest brother, Rich, in front of a flaming yellow, full-bloom forsythia bush outside the big, brick Lutheran church of my youth.

My mother, I think I'm remembering this correctly, wears a stylish dress she likely made herself and a round, white hat that, if turned upside down and used as a bucket, could easily hold a half-gallon of wild raspberries. Dad wears his Sunday uniform: suit, tie, and easy smile.

The occasion for the photo is telegraphed by what Rich wears. Dark trouser legs peek out from an angel-like gown whose yards of whiteness are broken only by his folded hands holding a black hymnal. It's Confirmation Sunday, either Palm Sunday or Easter Sunday 1965, and Rich is a newly minted communicant.

The formality of the photo shows just how important this day is for them. He's the firstborn, the pathfinder for the following five; likewise, their firstborn is moving toward high school and manhood. Together they stand atop one of life's important peaks and the pride of getting there shines through.

I also recall a tiny glint of satisfaction in Rich's eyes. It's a knowing sparkle, perhaps, to the fact that he survived eight years of Lutheran grade school and Luther's Small Catechism and now can shake the dust of both off his shoes forever.

It's a look you see only in youth, though, because none of us—Rich then, Peggy in 1966, David in 1967, me in 1969, Perry in 1971, and Christian in, ah, 1979?—ever did. Each may have thought Confirmation Sunday as parole day from catechism purgatory, but as our gray-haired elders predicted back then, it would become the first step on a journey of deeper understanding and deeper commitment.

As one of those gray-haired elders now, I confidently told a minute's-old confirmand last year that this day would become very important to him. Like me forty years earlier, the young man looked briefly at me as though I had one eye in the middle of my forehead and said, "Yeah, sure."

I remember more of that big day. I remember walking to our grandparents' house, just three blocks from the church, to a big party in Rich's honor. Grandma, apron already on, was stirring a roaster of gravy; Grandpa, suit coat already off, was stirring a whiskey sour for the gravy maker.

Aunts and uncles were everywhere and all slowly wandered into the living room where Rich, like a newly crowned Saxon prince, held court. All told him "how proud you must be" while revealing how proud they were (of what, I wondered, they hadn't done anything) and then handed him an envelope.

At dinner, of course, heaven's newest heir ate with the adults in the dining room while the rest of us unwashed whelps were sent to Siberia, the back room off the kitchen. It had no guards so, later, we snuck out the back door to enjoy spring. Rich, however, was trapped by another hour of dessert, coffee, and adult chatter.

I remember, too, Pastor Gross, our stony-faced minister and Grandpa's Missouri Synod soul mate, at the party. Every time I had seen him in church or at school, he was the stiff-collared, thunder-and-lightning voice of fear. That day, however, I saw and heard him laugh. Gee, pastors laughed?

Four years later, a photo was snapped of Mom, Dad, and me in front of that same flaming forsythia. I wear a flowing white gown, a black hymnal, and big smile; they, tired smiles and no hats. They had changed and I was about to. They knew it; I didn't.

Since I was a teenager I could not walk anywhere on the farm of my youth without thinking about the Native Americans who walked the same land before me. I wrote the following column after a spring visit to the farm in search of artifacts. Instead of beads and arrowheads, however, I found peace.

BOYS, BEADS, AND BEYOND
APRIL 10, 2011

As the Good Book rightly foretold, when I was a child I thought like a child and acted like a child. That means I did many foolish things.

Probably the most foolish thing I did was give away several tin cans filled with Native American artifacts that I had found in the fields of my family's southern Illinois dairy farm.

Well, I didn't exactly give 'em away. Some I sold, usually for a $1 a can. I once traded a to-the-brim can of beads, musket balls, rifle flints, and arrowheads for a pack of Juicy Fruit chewing gum that I knew cost a nickel.

Have I mentioned foolish?

Another time my brother David and I swapped some artifacts for two, well-used football helmets and shoulder pads from Southern Illinois University. Oh, they were the real deal—real leather, real Bakelite face guards, real cotton padding—as were we: really foolish.

The really dumb thing is that I still have the dumb helmet. I suppose I keep it to show just how galacticly stupid I was to hand over a Busch Bavarian (my father's brand then and now) can full of irreplaceable Native American history for two pieces of completely frivolous Americana.

That I had so many artifacts was no mystery. One June day my father came to the dinner table with a magnificent spear point. He had found it that morning while cultivating soybeans in the field just north of the farmstead. Cream-colored and maybe three inches long, it was extraordinary; the most remarkable thing I had ever seen.

A half-hour later, after Dad had moseyed off for his midday nap, I ran to the bean field. He was tired; I was afflicted. He rested; I never did. The search became the passion it remains, and forty-five years on, I still return to that field and to the search.

Success, then as now, is aided by the accident of birth. My family's farm, at the confluence of the Kaskaskia River with the Mississippi, has been known for generations as Indian Farm. The name extolled the land's Native tenants, the Kaskaskias, a tribe of the once-powerful Illinois Confederacy that, in the early 1700s, made their home in the flat, fertile Mississippi River bottoms.

Stand in the bare, late winter fields of Indian Farm today and you can see what drew the Kaskaskia to it. On its west is a long, shallow slough fed by the Mississippi that remains home to ducks, geese, muskrat, and beaver. In the distance, gray-barked pecan trees reach to the sky and continue to yield their

Like long-ago voices carried on the wind, Indian Farm's tall silos peek through a morning's early fog to suggest something more.

heavenly bounty every fall. Limestone bluffs rise to the north and two rivers crowd it on the east and south.

In fact, if not for the thatch of corn stalks at my feet and a picket of telephone poles marching steadily toward the levee, most of the land's native beauty remains. It's captivating and, often as not, I spend most of my too-brief visits listening for whispers of wisdom and lore rather than looking for arrowheads and beads.

What parts, I wonder, of the many lives that walked where I now stand remain hidden in the shadows of those grand pecan tress? Did the sight and smell of April's fresh earth move them to thank their Creator, too? Did the soft touch of a spring breeze also carry them gently and happily into a promising tomorrow?

For thirty-five years I have returned to Indian Farm, when I can, to replenish what it first gave me as a child. Now I return to listen, and look for beads and beauty and arrowheads and peace.

And one day, perhaps soon, I will return a final time to add my whisper to the eternal wind.

LESSONS LEARNED FROM TWENTY-TWO
TONS OF EDUCATION
APRIL 24, 2005

Today's southern breeze gently rustles the heavy-headed tulips outside my office window before sweeping through the apple tree to sprinkle a shower of blossom petals onto an emerald lawn.

A second later it picks me up on its warm wings and carries me back to the southern Illinois dairy farm of my youth. Back there, April brought two seasons: planting and baseball. Without fail, though, planting beat baseball because all hands, no matter their size or skill, were needed on the farm.

Mid-April usually planted me on the steel seat of an Oliver 77 that dragged a four-section spring harrow against the grain of our many fall-plowed fields.

Seat? I didn't sit. No one could as the narrow-front tractor bobbed like a cork from mellow plow slab to mellow plow slab slowly turning the bleached gray skin of that farm into a moist, jet-black bed of hope.

Despite the body-bruising, brain-rattling ride, I kept a keen but bouncing eye on the freshly turned soil of the previous pass for the telltale white of an arrowhead, rifle flint, and musket ball.

One of those precious finds, a cream-colored arrowhead, rests on my office desk today. It's a perfectly sculpted artifact of those long and long-gone days; a testament to the fact that while cultures come and go, only the land lasts forever.

My father would often be in an adjoining field, reworking my work with what was then a massive field cultivator, maybe sixteen feet wide. Not far behind him was the planter, manned by leathery, nearly always complaining Jackie, our farm's main hired hand.

Dad, of course, had the responsible job, applying the pre-plant herbicide and then working it in with the dirt-shaking cultivator. A homemade rig of steel saddle tanks, a PTO-driven pump, and hoses going everywhere made his 1850 Oliver look like something out of the Battle of the Bulge.

The spray only added a final, sinister touch: yolky-yellow Treflan for beans; milky white atrazine for corn.

Dad's rig easily outpaced Jackie's because the planter, a six-row ground-driven Oliver, was designed to break down. A whirl of sprockets, chains, and plates but no monitor, of course, it often tossed drive chains off its row units for no reason other than that was what it was engineered to do.

From afar, I could always tell when that happened. Jackie, upon discovering he had just planted five rows and not six for a half mile, would rub his three-day-old whiskers and fling fabulous curses into the wind. He hated that planter.

I, too, quickly learned to hate it the year I planted the farm's entire crop while on a Dean Warren Wessels–imposed college sabbatical. ("You're taking up a space for someone who actually wants to be here. Come visit me when you're serious about a world-class education.")

That was the same year, what with an excess of bone-headed, youthful labor at hand, Dad put the planter's tall and long dry fertilizer boxes back on. It meant more chains, more breakdowns, and more work. I toted, emptied, and then planted twenty-two tons of dry fertilizer, one fifty-pound sack at a time, that spring.

It was the education Dean Wessels somehow knew I needed because the next planting season found me back at the University of Illinois lifting myself and my young family forever out of the reach of spring harrows, saddle tanks, and Oliver planters.

And arrowheads, warm spring days in the field, and long evenings of quiet, tired satisfaction.

My and the lovely Catherine's return to Champaign carried a hidden bonus for Dad. Since he was destined to be the main corn planter the following spring, the main corn planter quickly became a shiny, new, monitored John Deere Max-Emerge.

Shortly thereafter, the fresh-air, log-wagon 1850 was traded for an air-conditioned Ford 9600 and the cranky Oliver baler was ditched for a Vermeer round baler. Guess Dad got an education during my final planting season, too.

Odd how an aching back can train an under-used brain, and apple blossom petals on a green sea can float you into yesterday.

PLANTING A SEED
MAY 5, 2013

The first good corn-planting day of spring finally arrived at my central Illinois farmette April 30. Like the month's previous twenty-nine days, however, no one within 100 miles used it to plant because near-record rains had washed April away.

So now it's May and it's late by any corn planting standard. On the southern Illinois dairy farm of my youth we sometimes finished planting corn in June, but we always started in April.

Those long ago planting seasons, all seasons, in fact, always marched to a two-step tune: the very predictable, twice-a-day milking of 100 Holsteins and the very unpredictable rise and fall of the nearby Mississippi River. The river was in God's hands; the cows in ours.

That meant the acres planted any day were limited to the acres Dad could "work"—field cultivate while applying a pre-plant herbicide—ahead of the planter between morning and evening milkings and then again at night. It wasn't much, usually fifty acres most days and maybe sixty in a big day and long night.

Jackie, the farm's loyal hired man, was the planter jockey. He worked 6:00 a.m. to 6:00 p.m. six days a week without fail. He had no watch because he couldn't tell time, but he did have three times—starting time, quitting time, and dinner time—programmed into his DNA and, like him, it never failed.

The Oliver 77 he drove was nearly as faithful. Gas-powered with both hydraulics and a PTO, it was his go-to tractor for planting, manure spreading, baling, and pulling grain and silage wagons. It ran like the watch Jackie didn't own.

The planter, an Oliver of mid-1960s vintage, was very different. It was the worst piece of engineered iron ever sold to anyone. It never completed one round, be it a quarter mile, a half mile or, like most of our fields, one mile, in a cornfield without some minor or major breakdown.

If, by some miracle, its chattering collection of ground-driven chains and rotating planter plates held together long enough to actually plant six rows up and back, Jackie, a world class cusser, could be seen on his knees in the middle of the headland praising the miracle.

Oh, the miracle wasn't on the level of Lourdes or Knock; it was bigger.

The planter stuck around as long as Jackie and my brothers and me. Since my father never ran it, he seemed to overlook the fact that its main design feature was failure. To him, most of the planter's failures were operator failures: we were going too fast or too slow; the ground was too wet or too dry; we wore our caps too low.

Huh?

As previous years' columns have detailed, the planter's final spring came in 1978. That cold, wet, forsaken season I planted every kernel, row, and acre with that forsaken planter.

But I was more than the corn planter that year; I also was the planter monitor. Four or five times every round, I climbed off the tractor to check every sprocket, chain, and planter box to make certain it could make it another 400 or so yards. If reassured, I'd climb back on the tractor and off I'd go.

For another 400 yards. Then I'd stop, climb down, and check it all again. Often on my way back to the tractor I'd smack the implement's tongue with a hammer just to let it know I still was alert.

Late that winter, I took a freezer full of food, a new interest in writing, and the lovely Catherine back to the Big U and off to a different future.

A couple of months later, my father, threatened with the prospect of planting corn with a machine he had fixed (and everyone else had cussed) daily for fifteen years, traded that planter for a six-row John Deere MaxEmerge with a Dickey-john monitor. Had he made the swap in 1978, I might have stayed.

Wait a minute, you don't think . . .

PRAYING AND WAITING
MAY 11, 2008

As the cold, wet planting season of 2008 slips into mid-May, corn and soybean farmers are grousing about weather delays, the likelihood of reduced yields, and a summer of stress before they find out if the former clobbered the latter.

While I empathize with their dilemma, that this is easily the most costly crop any farmer has ever planted and the delays only add to the historically high (until 2009, that is) tab, there truly is nothing to do but pray and wait.

While we weren't big on waiting on the southern Illinois dairy farm of my youth, we did pray. We gave thanks each morning for the new day; noontime dinners and evening suppers both began and ended with prayer and, after supper, the family always gathered for evening devotions (that concluded with two prayers) regardless of the season or undone chores.

In all that heavenly beseeching, though, I don't recall us ever praying for fair weather, a good crop, or high prices. Most times we thanked the Lord for the blessings we had received: caring friends, a crop-making July rain, good health, bountiful food, and respectfully suggested it would be fine with us if those blessings simply continued.

The heavy lifting, the formal, fervent praying, was left to the pastor during worship services. Since, as he sternly reminded us every Sunday, he was "a called and ordained servant of the Lord," I figured he had the singular ability, and maybe even the temporal responsibility, to make specific requests through prayer.

I mean, he often offered up names, dates, and ideas we simply didn't have the spiritual courage to pursue at the dinner table.

That cowardice began to drain from me, however, halfway through St. John's Lutheran School when my teacher that year, Mr. Hartman, told the story of a boy my age (what a coincidence!) saying the Lord's Prayer with hundreds of other churchgoers one Sunday morning.

As the group prayed, Mr. Hartman related solemnly, "The Lord heard only one voice, the voice of the young boy. Why? Because he was the only one in that church who was actually praying. The rest were just reciting words from memory while thinking about other things like baseball and fishing."

So that's how it works, I remember thinking; you have to mean what you say during prayer for prayer to be heard. It was a revelation, and it clearly explained why my parents bowed their heads and closed their eyes during our family devotions.

That reverence carried through my father's daily farming routine. I never heard him utter even the mildest of oaths despite the ample opportunities presented by the farm's many dimwitted hired men and its fleet of constantly breaking down machinery.

Once, when eyeing the latest hired hand–inspired disaster—either an overturned silage wagon or a telephone pole his Uncle Honey had plowed over, I can't remember which—I heard him mutter, "Well, you do what you can; the rest is up to the Lord."

In fact, the machinery-killing Uncle Honey was the inspiration of my father's favorite quasi-Biblical axiom. "The Lord protects fools and children," Dad often would say when he eyed Uncle Honey on a tractor. "That's a wonderful thing," he'd add, "because either way, Honey's covered."

More borderline blasphemous than sacred, I knew it wasn't a proper prayer. Still, it worked because in the twenty years Uncle Honey bent, busted, and beat up every piece of machinery he touched, not one hair on one person, including himself, was ever harmed by all the mayhem.

So, as you wait among your $250-per-bag seed watching mud dry on your unplanted, $6,000-per-acre land, pray. It's free, for heaven's sake.

IT WON'T KILL YOU
MAY 13, 2012

A drive through central Illinois one sunny, dry day last week featured miles of black earth, dozens of fast-moving tractors pulling wide, dust-chasing corn planters and soybean drills, and not one flatbed wagon or two-wheeled trailer holding that day's seed, fertilizer, or fuel.

The reason for those missing links is that, unlike the days of my farming youth, those links aren't missed. This year's fertilizer was put down last year and today's tractors, planters, and drills hold enough fuel and seed to lay a swath of corn or beans from here to tomorrow.

Not so on the southern Illinois dairy farm of my father and his wonderful Uncle Honey. In fact, back then backs seemed to move more farm inputs and outputs than all our tractors, wagons, augers, and combines combined. One story illustrates the essential logic of our farm's logistics.

Once, as I was carrying buckets of water to calves 100 or so yards from our house, a twice-daily chore, I asked my father why we didn't bury a water line to the calf barn.

"Why do that," he offered in his perpetually calm, measured voice, "when all I have to do is say, 'Alan, water the calves' and off you go for the buckets?"

Huh. The only thing simpler than his answer was me.

For many years, that same scheme applied to our handling of all the soybean meal used in our dairy feed rations. Since we owned one of the very first Mix-Mills, a long-ago brand for small, farm-based feed-making, we mixed soy meal with corn to grind (OK, automatically grind) feed every day.

The meal, however, arrived by rail boxcar twelve miles away. In burlap sacks. Bulging, 90 lb., burlap sacks.

That meant that on the big soybean meal day, every able-bodied man, boy, and dog traveled to the rail siding with tractors, hay wagons, and dread to drag, tote, and pack those monstrously heavy sacks for the slow ride to the farm.

Once there, of course, each was grappled by one man, or two boys, to the edge of the wagon to be opened and dumped into an auger that moved the meal to a ten-ton self-unloading bin that held it for later use.

During one of those sweat-soaked sessions I asked my father why everyone else had their bean meal delivered by truck and we instead wrestled sacks the size of Rhode Island. Again the answer was short, clear, and sensible: "It's cheaper this way."

Then he added the universal German Lutheran explanation for all the unnecessary sweat generated by farm folks since the Garden of Eden: "Besides, it doesn't kill us."

Really? That's a reason?

Hay season, of course, was the big back-breaker each year. We, however, doubled-down some of those hot, dusty summer weeks by also baling straw and emptying grain bins of the previous year's harvest.

Wheat straw was cotton candy compared to alfalfa hay, but emptying a grain bin in mid-June was a half-day sentence in hell. Since the used (of course)

2,200-bushel government bins required us to shovel more than 1,000 bushels to empty it, nothing on the farm was hotter, dirtier, or noisier than that awful job.

My father, no slack in him, usually handled one of the two scoop shovels required to keep the bin auger full. "Come on," he often urged me or one of my brothers, "it won't kill you."

I thought about his simple admonition for hard work last October as I packed thirty-five bags of concrete mix down two sets of steep stairs to a building project. Each bag seemed heavier than the one before and every step back up the stairs was.

But, you know what? It didn't kill me.

> *Bad habits usually ain't cheap. Several years ago, I dropped my two biggest vices within months of each other. Shortly thereafter, and thanks to those tweeting, techie children, I acquired a Kindle and more recently, an iPad, as well as digital subscriptions to* The New York Times *and* Wall Street Journal. *I've also acquired hours more each day to read, reflect, and proverbially reconnect. Talk about cheap.*

SILENCING THE CIRCUS
MAY 17, 2009

A month or so ago, the manager of this one-dog farmette clipped the coaxial cable that linked our rural home to the yellers at MSNBC, CNN, Fox, and the 264 other big-haired television airheads bloviating about other bloviators.

Our children, both fulfilling their destinies on the East Coast and therefore no part of the coming Great Silence, were stunned. What will you do for, like, Jon Stewart or Cardinal baseball, they asked.

Don't know, but once you've given up nicotine—I ended that torrid, thirty-five year love affair last August—you discover you can live pretty happily on four life-sustaining essentials: love, red meat, a couple of daily newspapers, and Guinness.

Somehow we managed to survive and thrive on less than that on the southern Illinois dairy farm of my youth. Even more shocking, we did it with only one television that received just four St. Louis stations. Pretty skinny menu for six children, two parents, an occasional live-in grandmother, a poodle, and Uncle Honey.

Our television, however, projected in color—two of 'em, in fact: black and white. The only person I knew who had a real color TV was Uncle Wally. (Once, during a visit to Uncle Wally's, we watched *Gunsmoke*'s Marshal Dillon walk into a gunfight wearing a pink Stetson. Lame hat notwithstanding, he drilled his opponent.)

To fill the colorless void of our upbringing, my brothers, sister, and I often played baseball in the nearby pasture, rode bikes, went fishing, searched the fields for arrowheads, built model cars, swam in the pond, hunted rabbits, quail, or squirrels, made and drove go-carts, and later rebuilt a super cool '47 Ford pickup.

In our spare time we baled hay, hauled silage, canned vegetables, milked cows, peeled potatoes, fed calves, cultivated corn, picked peas, washed windows, sowed alfalfa, and . . . well, we kept so busy we simply didn't have time to miss today's eyeball-grabbing, silence-shattering necessities like cable TV, cell phones, and iPods.

Despite this lack of 24/7 connectivity, I didn't know how disadvantaged we were until 1965 or so when I spent a weekend at my friend's 160-acre tenant farm. Its house had a wood cookstove and no bathroom.

But the farm did sport chickens, pigs, a Jersey milk cow, a small flock of almost-pet sheep, some beef cows, a nicely appointed outhouse, and a working windmill.

Who needed television when there were chickens to chase, sheep to ride, and a windmill to climb? It was easily the best weekend of my young life.

Sometime in the late 1960s, a tiny black-and-white portable TV sprouted in the corner of our big farm kitchen. It was less to entertain my mother during the day—Oprah? What's an Oprah?—than to keep my father, and later we boys, company when we ate supper alone after the evening milking.

That TV, far more than the one in the family room, became our window on the world. On it I saw Jack Nicklaus win his fourth, slate gray jacket at the 1972 Master's, watched Archie Bunker's pasty face darken when he yelled at his meathead son-in-law, and witnessed Sen. Sam Ervin shake his Deputy Dog jowls at Watergate conspirators.

Looking back, my guess is media scholars will likely peg that time, not today, as television's premier age. We were a better informed, better entertained, and far-less divided nation before today's satellite monkeys began their circus acts.

After all, if I want to see a circus, I'll buy a ticket, and if I want the news, I'll buy more newspapers. With the $780 a year I'm not sending to some nicotine-ingesting media titan, I can afford both.

Easter morning, 1962 or 1963. Our parents gave us boys a box load of baseball equipment to properly rejoice in our Savior's Resurrection. We were so proud that we took it all to church, then to Grandpa and Grandma's backyard for this portrait. Left to right: me with the glove and ball, my brother David pounding the catcher's mitt, my brother Richard ready to swing the bat, and my sister Peggy, standing. My brother Perry kneels next to our first cousin Susan. Peggy and Susan seemed quite happy to distance themselves from our excitement.

ANY DAY IN MAY
MAY 22, 2011

When you're young and farm-born, May isn't so much a month as a carnival; a pleasant stretch that's no longer spring but not quite summer, a time heavy with little more than possibilities.

On the southern Illinois dairy farm of my youth, May was a corner-turner, the swing month of both the farm and my family's year. The eventual success of what mattered most to us, October's corn yields and the Cardinals' season, was usually measured by that month's yardstick.

Back then, a good May would bring a timely rain but no mud, a couple of Bob Gibson–pitched shutouts, a no-work Sunday or two, and a meal of fried ham, wilted garden lettuce, and potato pancakes.

Almost fifty years later that would still be a good May.

I remember the farm gained tempo as the month gained days. May meant corn planting and that meant my father saddling the farm's biggest tractor, an Oliver 1850, with plumbed-together, shop-built sprayer tanks. The homely pair carried milky atrazine for corn and egg-colored Treflan for beans in a pre-plant attack on the farm's impressive weed population.

The big rig (well, relatively so, the field cultivator wasn't as wide as today's bass boats are long, and the 1850 packed only half as much horsepower) preceded hired man Jackie piloting a steady, slow Oliver 770 and a six-row, ground-driven Oliver planter.

The planter's pace, no more than 4 mph, suited steady, slow Jackie. The permanently tanned, usually swearing man possessed the unique talent of looking busy, even sweating, while using ninety minutes to do sixty minutes of work. (His younger brother, Orlie, however, didn't own the same gift.)

Planting also featured my two older brothers and me scrapping over who would join Dad and Jackie in the field, assist herdsman Howard with the evening milking, or help Mom in the garden. The first two jobs paid fifty cents an hour, the latter nothing. The former two were exhilarating; the latter awful. Brothers Rich and Dave often rotated between barn and field; I rotated between hilling potatoes and hoeing peas.

But late May always brought enough farm work to free me from vegetable purgatory. There was corn to rotary hoe, beans to finish planting, cows to milk, and 80 or so acres of lush, emerald green alfalfa to cut, crimp, rake, bale, haul, and stack.

The work gave Rich, Dave, and me two great gifts: we spent all day with the farm's rough cut men and we each pocketed a slick $6 or so for work we probably would have done for free.

The only drawback to hay heaven was that it often meant Memorial Day was also Alfalfa Day. More times than not, just as A. J. Foyt and Mario Andretti began their screaming drives around the big oval of the Indianapolis 500, my brothers and I were slowly, slowly circling a big hayfield with slow, slow Jackie.

For a decade beginning in 1965, the last week of May usually delivered a grade school, high school, or college graduation ceremony for one of my siblings or me. A quick count suggests I attended at least ten and maybe twelve of these events, yet I can't recall one ceremony, one speaker, or one post-diploma party.

I do, however, remember that on my high school graduation day we seniors practiced the ceremony in the morning, then played the traditional senior-faculty softball game. I have no idea who won, but I know I was home, rotary hoeing corn, by 2:00 p.m.

Dull boy? Probably, but I remember it being such a fine May day that I wanted to just be on the farm and in the field.

Most May days, I still do.

SUMMER

GROW

Summer always seemed like one big, steaming kitchen on Indian Farm. Oh, we spent hours, days, and weeks in my mother's kitchen cooking big noon dinners, canning the coming winter's vegetables, and baking, baking, and baking. But to me and my brothers, summer was a time for cooking up all sorts of things on the farm: tree houses in the big silver maples that circled the house, homemade go-karts that required the use of Dad's welder and the three-horsepower motor from Mom's garden tiller, a tippy wooden raft to float among the cows wading in the mud-bottomed pond. Soon enough, though, we graduated from childhood fun to fields of work and wages. Not a bad trade, really, because while the money is long spent, the memories linger.

CLEANING THE PLATE
JUNE 3, 2007

On the southern Illinois dairy farm of my youth, the beginning of summer marked the kick-off of a season of great food. Like Roman soldiers of yore, we, the small legion of family farm workers—my Uncle Honey, father, mother, four brothers, sister, and I—worked at eating so we could eat into the ever-ending work on the farm's 720 acres and 100 Holsteins.

That meant the kitchen crew—my mother, sister, and we boys still too short to reach a tractor's clutch pedal—worked harder than the field crew. Five meals a day, six days a week was always on the menu: breakfast, a mid-morning lunch for the morning milkers, dinner at noon, a mid-afternoon snack for the evening milkers, then supper.

Actually, it was six meals a day. The evening milk crew, usually my father and one of us boys, ate late by ourselves after the cows were tended. That was hours after the rest of the family had shared supper and evening devotions.

The only break from the dawn-until-after-dark regime came on Sunday. Breakfast that day was coffee cake or cinnamon rolls before church, noon dinner at one of the sets of grandparents', and supper was "get it yourself" back home.

The season began with the same late-spring meal each year. The key was garden-fresh Bibb lettuce. The lettuce, picked when it was half the size of a child's hand, then tossed with a vinegar dressing, was the perfect complement to a meal of potato pancakes, applesauce, and fried ham.

It was a once-a-year event because, I always figured, grating a peck of potatoes to make enough pancakes to fill nine people took hours.

(The saddest phone call home now is when, usually by chance, I telephone my parents to chat and my father happily relates, "Just finished a big meal of potato pancakes, fried ham, and fresh lettuce. You'd have loved it.")

Those noon dinners featured equal parts of love, flavor, and sweat. The anchor was some cut of beef or pork. Usually it was a nicely baked beef roast or a well-peppered, heavily salted pork roast. Variations included pork sausage, salted pork, pork chops, liver, meatloaf, or 100 other meat dishes my mother, with no recipe other than memory, magically delivered.

Then came the vegetables, as in plural because all Germans are born with an unshakeable belief they will not make it to heaven if they don't eat at least two, three is even better insurance, vegetables at every meal.

Green beans, sweet corn, radishes, onions, asparagus, leaf lettuce, red beets, creamed spinach, creamed Swiss chard, coleslaw, sauerkraut, kohlrabi, Brussels sprouts, peas, and the queen mother of summer gardens, tomatoes.

And, of course, potatoes. Boiled potatoes, baked potatoes, mashed potatoes, creamed potatoes, sweet potatoes. And all afloat in a sea of gravy or butter or both.

Rare was the dinner that didn't finish with cake, fruit or pudding pies (another German Lutheran rule: if you're making pie, you're making two kinds of pie), fresh fruit, cookies, and other sweet treats my mother knew we'd die for.

My noon meal always ended with a slice of buttered bread topped with a massive load of homemade peach, apple, strawberry, grape, or blackberry jelly. Always.

Then, surprise, the adults napped until 1:00 p.m. My father and mother always went to their bedroom; Uncle Honey to a webbed chaise lounge on the porch where the sports section of the *St. Louis Globe-Democrat* slowly drifted lower and lower until it covered his closed eyelids and open mouth.

Now, as summer again seeps back into farm country, I'd give nearly anything to sneak back to that farm and that table for a week's worth of that homegrown pleasure.

A short time before I wrote this column, the weekly newspaper of my distant hometown carried the obituary of a former hired man on Indian Farm. He was a part-timer who worked full-time on the summer hay crew. He was, and will remain, forever thin, tanned, and smiling.

SUMMERTIME MEANT HAY TIME
JUNE 6, 2004

On the southern Illinois dairy farm of my youth, Memorial Day marked summer's official beginning. School was finished, the weather warm, and fieldwork, aside from a fast rotary hoeing of just-emerged corn, was light.

Most Memorial Days meant a day in town at Grandma and Grandpa's home. After a noon meal of barbecued chicken, coleslaw, potato salad, and several cold Falstaffs, the grown-ups would watch the Indianapolis 500 on Grandpa's new-fangled TV while we kids rounded up a pick-up game of softball that rarely ended before dark.

The next day, May 31—remember?—the summer work season began. Down home that meant making hay. Rare was the May that didn't end without hay season beginning.

And with more than 100 or so hungry Holsteins to feed four and five times a day for the next year, that meant months of sweet-smelling, sweat-inducing alfalfa hay bales.

My brothers and I assimilated into the hay crew slowly. The first summer our legs were long enough to reach the tractor clutch was spent, at fifty cents an hour, dragging a seven-foot, ground-driven New Idea rake around and around the hayfield making real work—fluffy single, double, even triple windrows—for real men.

The next summer we handed down the raking to a younger brother and headed to the hay shed. The tin pole barn that held our precious feed was more than 100 feet long, 40 feet wide, and 20 feet tall; a dark sweatbox that held heat better than hay.

Finally, at about thirteen years old, we graduated to the wagon, first snagging bales out of the jerking Oliver baler to drag back to the man stacking the wagon. By watching him, we learned how to tie the load, bale-by-bale and rick-by-rick, so it arrived at the hay shed intact. By that summer's end, we were stacking bales solo.

Before my brothers and I made it to the top of the haying heap, though, the hard-bodied, less nimble-minded hired men did the work. And they worked like dogs, usually panting and always yapping.

One, Charlie G., was the strongest bundle of muscle I've ever seen. When unloading wagons in the barn, Charlie often grabbed the twin twines of an eighty-pound alfalfa bale in each hand to throw the green monsters at you like two shot puts. In the field, he'd stack the wagons seven and eight bales high.

Charlie also was the only man I've ever known to install a floor shifter in a '55 Ford coupe with just an adjustable wrench and an ax. The wrench for the bolts; the ax to cut a hole in the floorboard. He also once bit a cow on the ear, but that's another story.

Howard, who longtime readers of this column may remember as Hoard the Dairyman, originally came to the farm as a hay hand. His three younger brothers worked on the farm (only one of them, the smallest, Jackie, made the grade), so Howard was given a try-out after my grandfather bailed him out of the state mental institution in Anna.

Howard was uncomplaining and unwearying; he also was undeserving of his fifteen years in Anna. While milking one winter evening years later, Howard related that his father had had him "committed" after they fought over money.

"That's just the way it was back then," he said as casually as you'd tie your shoe.

Although he was a big man, his meek manner hid his great might. One morning when our motley crew of boys, men, and whiners were picking up bales in the field, Charlie pulled his bale-in-each-hand trick and tossed two bales onto the wagon effortlessly.

Howard, I guess, thought he needed to speed up to keep his $1-an-hour job, so he grabbed two bales in each hand and tossed them just as easily onto the wagon. The work stopped as we dug the stacker out of a grave of alfalfa.

Charlie never pulled his trick again and, without a word, neither did Howard.

Today, square alfalfa hay bales are a rare and valuable commodity. So are the men of the hayfields of my youth.

DAIRYMAN'S MONTH
JUNE 21, 1997

Since 1939, June has been America's official "Dairy Month." This invention of advertising held little charm or meaning for me on the southern Illinois dairy farm of my youth. To me, every month was dairy month.

Our dairy began modestly in the mid-1950s, a temporary tie-stall parlor in a drafty wooden barn under an ancient pecan tree. The main machinery in that original barn was buckets and hired men. Buckets for milk, buckets for feed, hired men to tote the buckets.

Soon, a new parlor was completed and the herd size doubled. The milking machines, glass pipeline, and 1,000-gallon bulk tank made the work easier and more sanitary, but the extra cows required as much labor as before.

The 100-cow milking string had special manpower requirements. One person worked full-time at the dairy to milk, feed, clean up, bed, and milk. The twice-a-day milkings also required a second man, usually my father, to assist with the dawn and dusk chore.

And a third person was needed to milk part-time so that the full-time man and Dad could have one day off per week. This person usually was a field hand who Dad reckoned possessed enough brain cells to operate the parlor's technical equipment.

But as every dairyman knows, cow-loving laborers are hard to find and even harder to keep. Our farm was no exception; we were always in the labor market. That meant we usually took the first guy who drifted in. We then attempted to mold him into a herdsman. It rarely succeeded.

The first full-time dairy hand I remember was Bob H. Old and slow best described Bob. Milking took forever because Bob took forever to do anything. And he never walked. Bob drove the dairy's sputtering Ford loader tractor everywhere, even when getting the cows from the pasture or going the two hundred yards to his house for lunch.

Around Christmas 1964, Bob, like most of the farm's hired hands, left without giving notice. One Monday morning he simply failed to show up.

Into the void stepped Monroe W., a scrawny, toothless piece of tanned Missouri leather who gummed Red Man, always packed a loaded .22 pistol in his right boot, and could never be found when sweat-producing work threatened. Like Bob before him, Monroe and his faux southern belle wife loaded their car one night and drove south, we reckoned, and out of our lives.

Next was Bill H., who arrived one hot June noon in a purple, air-conditioned '65 Ford Galaxy. It was the first such equipped car I'd seen and I asked Dad how a hired hand could afford that luxury and we couldn't.

I don't recall Dad's mumbled answer, but I do remember him saying Bill came highly recommended. "He doesn't smoke, drink, or swear."

Within days, of course, Bill was relating hundreds of explicit stories to a rapt, adolescent audience: my brothers and me. He also sneaked beer into the dairy

Even vacations included cows. My father snapped this photo while he and Mom toured California dairies in the late 1960s. I'm not sure what impressed Dad more about this set-up—the outdoor feed bunk or the well-mannered cattle. Indian Farm didn't have either.

barn on Dad's days off and taught us how to roll cigarettes. And one steamy August evening, Bill fired up his cool Ford and vanished.

Howard replaced, easily replaced, Bill. Howard was a gentle, quiet bear who had two built-in advantages over other potential herdsmen: he already was the weekend relief milker so he knew the regime, and he could read.

Howard ended most of the annual hiring and subsequent sneaking off. He stayed twenty-five years, which means he remained three years after the barns, silos, and parlor were emptied for the September 1989 auction that ended dairying on the farm.

No one ever spoke of the shared loyalty and love that grew between Howard and my family over that quarter century of mutual need, but plainly that's what it was.

Finally, old and ill and with no pension except for a few Social Security nickels every month, Howard left the farm. He went by car, too, but Dad was the driver this time as he ferried Howard to the hospital where, soon and sadly, alone, he died.

I recall only a handful of the thousands of cows that paraded through that parlor over the years. Yet I remember many of the tiniest details of every one of the dozens of men who worked there.

June shouldn't be Dairy Month; June should be Dairyman's Month.

This is the first of several Uncle Honey columns that, through the years, highlighted the metal-bending, tree-snapping, burn-down-the-barn farming career of my beloved great uncle. Honey was, truly, one-of-a-kind, and readers from Wyoming to Washington, D.C., have smiled and smiled when asking me if he was indeed real. Real? Hey, my father still has the heartburn to prove it.

A HONEY OF A MAN
JUNE 23, 1996

June heat slinks into farm country to fuel growing crops, late afternoon laziness, and thirty-year-old summertime memories.

Back then, the farm of my youth was big by anyone's standard: 100 or so dairy cows; 100 acres of alfalfa; and over 700 acres of corn, soybeans, and wheat.

And it swallowed manpower like kids gulp soda. No matter how many men— or, in the case of my brothers and me, boys—you threw at it, the work never seemed done.

One summer, when I was about eight years old, my great uncle showed up to help. He had sold his milk route in town a couple of months before to retire to a life of fishing, listening to Cardinal baseball, and gardening.

By mid-June of that first retirement summer, the garden was planted, the Cardinals were in last place, and the fish had stopped biting. So he drove to the farm and announced he was ready to assist in any way he could.

My father was not anxious to hire his Uncle Honey.

That's right; Honey. It was a childhood nickname given to a thoughtful, sweet-natured boy who, as he grew into the town's easygoing milkman and then as a gentle, older man, never outgrew it.

He was a honey of a man, too: quiet, unpretentious, imperturbable. If a bad thought ever crossed his mind, it never crossed his lips.

Yet Dad had serious reservations about his kind uncle's offer. He had worked for Honey as a boy on the milk route and the thing he remembered most about those early mornings was Honey's deep belief that the clutch of a delivery truck was an unnecessary appendage, a waste of iron and engineering.

To Dad, an owner of a fleet of farm machinery, most of it with clutches, Honey's indifference to things mechanical spelled trouble.

But there was little Dad could do. He needed the help and Honey wanted to help. There would be no argument, for Honey did not argue. Ever.

My father's instincts, though, quickly proved accurate. Two weeks into his new job, Uncle Honey sprung a six-row, rear-mounted cultivator beyond repair when he snagged a pecan tree stump while laying-by corn.

It was a hint of greater carnage to come. In subsequent years, Honey became the only man I ever knew to:

- plow out a telephone pole;
- break a cast iron hand throttle off an Oliver 77 trying to give it more gas;
- unsuccessfully pump a crowbar up a fifty-foot silo by putting it in a howling silage blower;
- nearly bury a sixteen-foot iron gate and its railroad tie gatepost with, what had been only moments before, a rather good five-bottom IH plow;
- put a pliers over my father's fingers to "help" Dad hand-tighten a nut, and
- flip two, full Gehl silage wagons during the same week.

My father never let Honey near the combine, cows, or corn planter.

The irony in all these feats was that a milder, kinder, more soft-spoken man never walked a barnyard. Honey was the same calm ocean after his greatest moments of grand destruction as he was before.

Thirteen Junes ago, and nearly twenty years of machinery mayhem after he first arrived on the farm, Uncle Honey died quietly and peacefully.

I received word of his passing on the eve of lengthy trip I was about to take as a national magazine editor. Regrettably, I did not cancel the trip to return home to say a final goodbye to a truly great uncle.

But I have the memories and they bubble up every summer as the heat of June ripples across the horizon to rattle the corn and the past.

Besides, it's impossible to forget the explosion made by a silage blower when its paddles, roaring at 2,000 rpm, attempt to eat a crowbar Uncle Honey had mislaid on the unloading apron of a silage wagon.

HEEEE'S BAAAACK: UNCLE HONEY PART II
MAY 31, 1998

Two Junes ago, this weekly effort recalled past summers spent with my father's darling, but dangerous, Uncle Honey. Honey, you may recall, was a case study in human irony. On his feet he was incredibly imperturbable; on a tractor seat he was death personified.

After that first Honey alert was published, readers throughout the U.S. wrote or called to tell me about their Uncle Honeys. Most related funny tales of relatives who possessed the Honey-like gift of destroying massive amounts of farm machinery through careful inattention to small things like telephone poles, barns, and rivers.

The stories were good, and a few even stood a chance of topping the woe begotten by my kind, iron-bending uncle. Yet, in the interest of protecting the Honey franchise—hey, I invented it, remember?—I must respectfully suggest that no one will ever out-Honey my Honey.

Fact is, as Honey would say, I was only at half-throttle in the first column.

Had I opened 'er up a bit, I'd have told of the time my father had me tote a jug of drinking water to Uncle Honey who, with an 1850 Oliver and fourteen-foot disk, was ripping up a distant pasture for reseeding. After I delivered the water, Honey asked me to ride a few rounds on the tractor's flat fender so we could share our common passion: the St. Louis Cardinals. I hopped aboard.

As we completed the first dusty round and approached the field's shiny new five-strand barbed wire fence, Cardinal-talking Honey madly spun the steering wheel left as he stomped on the left rear wheel brake. The tractor, against every Newtonian law of nature, snapped 180 degrees left like a spring-loaded hinge.

In the dusty commotion of the emergency—really, typically Honey—turn, the right rear disk gang snagged the bottom strand of the fence's barbed wire and like a big green fishing reel, began to wrap it around the gang. As we sped back across the lumpy fescue pasture, the disk kept pulling wire off successive posts and the gang kept gobbling it up.

"Uncle Honey!" I screamed over the roar of the tractor, "you hooked the bob-wire!"

"Huh?" he said passively as he twisted around to eye the straightest, most taut strand of wire you ever saw chasing us down the field.

"Ahhh," he noted after the quick survey, "it's almost to the corner post. It'll break then." And sure enough, the wire did break at the corner post.

Honey knew things like that.

Uncle Honey on the Kaskaskia River speeding for the great, wide Mississippi sometime in the late 1970s. No surprise that he's alone in the boat's stern. No one in that boat, or southern Illinois, trusted him to drive.

Another time I was in the front passenger seat of his land yacht Pontiac when the car slipped off a skinny, rain-slickened field road. In classic Honey fashion, however, the car's right front wheel was in the road's shallow left ditch and the right rear wheel was in the opposite ditch.

Having never been in a car that was perpendicular to the road, I thought we were in a bad fix. If Honey thought the same, he never let on. He just gunned the big V-8 and we kept on motoring.

After a minute or so of corn splattering my side of the windshield while the Pontiac's rear-end took out part of the field's end rows, Uncle Honey looked over to me and, as if imparting some ancient Tibetan wisdom, said quietly, "The secret's not to stop."

That was it. The secret's not to stop.

He didn't and we didn't and we floated right down that greasy road as if on rails.

Space doesn't allow me to relate the exact circumstances of how Honey later smashed my family's car with a semi-mounted plow one October Sunday. But I can say it had something to do with not stopping.

Nor do I have time to describe the look on a hired man's face when the poor soul found his thumbs inside the bead of a tire—because Honey had told him to put 'em there to keep the inner tube from pinching as he pumped air into it—at the exact instant the tire popped into its rim seat.

I can only tell you that until that day I didn't know it was humanly possible for one person to hold up a twelve-ply, sixteen-inch wagon tire and rim with just two thumbs.

And then take off running with it.

No, against most every lesson taught me by my unique great uncle, I won't go full throttle with my best Honey stories because I reckon some people may try to out-Honey me again. Go ahead; let 'er rip.

After all, the secret's not to stop.

ACTUALLY, JUNE WAS CULTIVATOR MONTH
JUNE 6, 2010

Yes, of course, June is Dairy Month.

And National Ice Tea Month, National Candy Month, National Soul Food Month, National Smile Month, and National Turkey Lovers Month.

With 100 or so Holsteins on the farm of my youth, however, each year, month, week, and day started and ended with dairy, so June by any other name—National Rose Month, National Rivers Month, National Accordion Awareness Month—was still June.

In fact, the month's only monotony-breaking feature back then was cultivating; June was cultivating month on our farm. First, the corn was carefully weeded, tilled, and hilled, then the beans, then the corn again.

We called that second corn cultivation "laying-by," as in "We laid-by the corn this week." That meant the year's tillage for that crop was done.

I don't know where the term originated but I do know two things about laying-by corn. First, it never meant the weeds laid down; Dad always followed the last cultivator pass with a 2,4-D soaking a week or so later.

Second, we didn't lie down either. No sooner had all the cultivating been completed, there was wheat to cut, straw to make, and oftentimes during straw season, a cutting of sweet-smelling alfalfa to sweat and swear over, too.

All these tasks had two common elements: mostly Oliver equipment and always my great Uncle Honey. Dad's quiet, easygoing uncle, retired from his milkman route in town, was king of the cultivator and prince of the seven-foot sickle mower.

Indeed, when Honey drove off the farmlot with either a cultivator or mower, weeds trembled, alfalfa wept, and every air-sucking man or beast within two miles feared for their lives.

It wasn't that Honey was a spiteful or hurtful man interested in inflicting pain. On the contrary, his nickname said it all. As a youth, Honey was so sweet-natured, and OK, a bit slow of foot, that his mother called him Honey-this and Honey-that. The name quickly replaced his given name, Lorenz.

Sweet, kind, and quiet though he was, Honey's biggest blind spot was mechanical skill. He lacked it. Entirely. Moreover, he didn't care how machinery worked as long as it worked. Which, with Honey at the helm, usually wasn't for long.

For example, when Dad made the switch from four-row-wide to six-row-narrow farming, our two ancient, mounted Oliver cultivators were replaced with one, six-row, rear-mounted Case cultivator. It was a thing of beauty; wide, orange, shiny, and stout, it all but screamed 1964.

Then Honey climbed in the tractor's cushioned seat that first day. Two hours later, the tractor, cultivator, and driver were back in the farmlot with the driver complaining to my father that the new cultivator didn't work because it had begun to "plow out rows."

Dad, long aware of his uncle's machinery murdering skills, took one look down the cultivator's big, 6×6 main beam and saw it had been bent. Badly.

My father hung his head. Not even one morning into its young life and our brand-new cultivator had received the Honey Treatment: Honey had managed to "spring it," bending its central beam badly enough to cause one side, or "just three rows" he noted in his quiet manner, to track into the corn rows and not alongside 'em.

I heard my father mumble something about his uncle "setting a personal record" for breaking a new piece of equipment. "Just three hours" he repeated twice.

Honey, true to his name, however, acted as though he didn't hear Dad. He had that gift and it often came in handy, especially most Junes.

Maybe next June—remind me, will you?—I'll tell you about Honey and sickle mowers.

The following column was awarded Story of the Year from the American Agricultural Editors' Association. I can still see my father's face immediately after it happened, now more than fifty years ago.

SUMMERTIME ON THE FARM: ARE YOUR CHILDREN SAFE?
JUNE 18, 1995

It happened on May 31, 1964, in a weed-choked cornfield, thousands of green, straight rows from the farmhouse. The boy was a month short of his ninth birthday; his father, closing in on forty. Neither foresaw trouble.

Because of the spring in the kid's legs, the father had asked the boy to accompany him while cultivating. "The corn is thick with sweet potato vines," the man explained. "Yesterday I climbed off and on this tractor a hundred times to clear them from the cultivator. Today, you'll do the climbing and the clearing."

And the boy did, dozens of times in the first few rounds. Each tug-of-war with the vines on the rear-mounted cultivator meant the boy had to climb down, then up the man-sized steps forward of the big Case tractor's left rear wheel. Soon he too was tired of the big steps.

Finally, to avoid the steps, the boy clambered onto the tractor's drawbar to ride it until the next inevitable stop. His feet found a purchase: left foot on part of the drawbar assembly, right foot on a nearby piece of flat, solid iron. The father watched patiently.

The boy then said, "This'll work. Let's go." The father pushed the hydraulic lever to release the single action cylinder that held up the cultivator. Instantly the massive cultivator dropped, and just as swiftly, the boy screamed.

The flat, solid iron surface where the youngster had placed his right foot was the cast iron base of the vertical cylinder. When the cultivator dropped, the boy's foot was smashed between it and the cylinder's stop plate.

It was an accident; serious, yet not life-threatening. The boy would lose two toes and a summer of baseball. The father would lose faith in himself. How could he have placed his young son in harm's way?

It happens all the time. According to the National Farm Medicine Center (NFMC) in Marshfield, WI, an estimated 300 children die in farm and ranch accidents each year. For every death, claims NFMC, forty-two other farm kids are hospitalized and 1,120 more children require emergency room care.

None are planned. Each makes little sense. Every one causes pain. Pain of the flesh that, if the child survives, will heal; and pain of the heart that, if the child dies, will never heal.

Marilyn Adams knows that pain. In late 1986, her eleven-year-old son Keith suffocated in a gravity flow wagon of corn after he had been assigned to watch it unload on their Iowa farm. He was alone; no one knows why he climbed into the wagon.

A year later, Adams launched Farm Safety 4 Just Kids, a non-profit organization that alerts and informs parents and children alike of farm dangers. Currently, the group has forty-four chapters and over 2,000 members across the U.S. and Canada.

This past winter and spring, Farm Safety 4 Just Kids produced a haunting, effective farm safety campaign. The four-color, full-page ads ran in several issues of *Successful Farming* magazine.

Each page features the smiling, gap-toothed face of a single girl or boy killed in a recent farm accident. An accompanying box contains information about the forever-young child's name, age, career ambition, cause of death. Shawn W. Petersen died, one ad states starkly, when the twelve-year-old was "Caught in a sweep auger."

The children's parents provided the photos and the brief biographies to offer you the easy lesson they learned in the cruelest way: all the promise and hope contained in your child's smile is as fleeting as their next heartbeat unless you keep them safe.

My father learned the lesson that sunny May day long ago. I will never forget the look of utter horror on his face as I screamed when that fat cylinder smashed my foot. And I will never forget that I did not cry. Nor will I forget that he did.

I suppose that's the way it always is when a child dies needlessly in a farm accident. Parents are the only ones left to cry.

ALL-STAR SEASON
JUNE 21, 2009

As the end of June edges into sight, my mind floats back to those hot, long days on the southern Illinois dairy farm of my youth when noon dinner brought everyone together for the day's big meal. Afterwards, all the adults napped until precisely 1:00 p.m.

Uncle Honey, my father's uncle who spent twenty of his retirement years breaking machinery on our farm, didn't nap so much as doze.

Every day Honey reclined in a chaise lounge on the screened-in porch off the kitchen to read the sports section of the *St. Louis Globe-Democrat*. Shortly after he began, though, the paper would noiselessly descend until it covered his face. If the caw from a distant crow awakened him, the reading-sinking-dozing process began anew.

The memory is very vivid because I wanted to read the sports section. I never dreamed of pre-empting Honey's seniority, but I often wondered why his slumber couldn't be induced by other, less secular journals like the *Lutheran Witness* or *Hoard's Dairyman*.

To my great surprise, Honey knew of my newspaper envy. In 1966, I spent a roasting, mid-July week at Lutheran camp. (Camp Wartburg was aptly named, we were told, for the Saxon castle the Great Reformer hid in to avoid his own grilling by some close-minded papists.) When I returned home, the week's worth of sports sections were waiting for me. Honey had saved 'em.

It was especially wonderful because baseball's All-Star game had been played in St. Louis while I was at the no-radio, no-newspaper camp reading the book of Jonah.

Honey did other wonderful favors for my two older brothers and me. Since he and his wife were parents of two, older daughters, he adopted Richard, David, and me when he wanted to have some father-son fun.

For example, one summer dinner Uncle Honey casually informed my mother that "if the boys can be cleaned up by 3 o'clock," he'd take us to St. Louis for the ballgame that night. It must have been in 1964 or '65 because the game was at old Sportsman's Park, near today's St. Louis University.

At 3:00 p.m. my brothers and I shined like new pennies and off we went in Honey's '49 Chevy, first to his house where Aunt Esther was waiting with a light supper, then on to St. Louis where Honey never waited at one stop sign.

I remember only two things about that game. First, when we arrived near the ballpark, Honey drove into the back alley of some nearby tenements. When we stopped, a well-dressed black man—one of the first African Americans I ever saw—walked calmly from a building's sagging back stoop to the car. Honey nodded, gave him a dollar bill, and parked the car.

The second thing I recall is that the game went extra innings, fourteen if memory serves. As we walked into the dark-as-a-cave alley after midnight, I was shaking like a leaf. Not Honey; he never appeared worried, not even after he plowed out a telephone pole or rolled an overloaded silage wagon onto its side.

When we neared the car a voice from the darkness said, "Long one tonight."

"Yep," replied Honey as he handed the man another dollar, "see ya in a couple of weeks." And off we went to run more Missouri stop signs.

On July 14th the All-Star game returns to St. Louis for the first time since, well, I last looked at the book of Jonah. That day I'll be thinking about Uncle Honey, his private ballgame parking spot, and those big, red signs he insisted only suggested we stop.

'Course I'll do all that as I read the sports section during a nap.

MY HIGH-TECH TEENS
JUNE 24, 2007

About the time I broke the cotton shackles of my mother's apron strings for the glorious freedom of my father's fields, a technology wave hit the southern Illinois dairy farm of my youth.

The exact year of the surge escapes me, but I remember its first hint: the purchase of a green-as-money, six-row, thirty-inch Oliver corn planter.

The switch from a "four-row-wide" cropping pattern, (four rows spaced forty inches apart, or the width of a horse), to "six-row-narrow" boosted one person's productivity fifty percent in every field operation, and substantially increased yields.

It also brought change after change.

Out went the front-mounted, two-row cultivators; in came one, rear-mounted, six-row cultivator. Out went the small, wooden dump wagons; in came two, 100-bushel, self-unloading wagons. Out went a clanking Kewanee drag elevator; in came a shiny, fifty-foot long, six-inch in diameter auger.

Then, just before one year's wheat harvest, the final proof of our farm's progress arrived: an International Harvester 303 combine.

We already owned a tiny, self-propelled (remember that phrase?) Massey-Harris combine, but the IH was an enormous leap upward: an eighty-bushel grain tank, eleven-foot wide grain head, and twice the horsepower of that toy-like Massey. Wow.

During that same era Dad invested in two other pieces of then-high-capacity, high-efficiency equipment few local farmers owned or even had seen.

The first was a Hahn Hi-Boy, a self-propelled, 250-gallon sprayer. It resembled a seven-foot-tall orange tricycle and was powered by a twenty-or-so horsepower Wisconsin engine mounted directly in front of the operator and atop the rigid frame of the hinged front (and only) drive wheel.

My father, Richard Guebert, Sr., explaining the workings of a new stave manure silo to visitors of our farm's open house in the mid-1970s. It was Dad's idea; an above-ground unit complete with an underground pumping system. Despite many claiming that it would never work, the silo worked perfectly until Dad, and the cows, retired twenty years later.

It was a doddering, ugly, albeit innovative beast with never-before-seen features like adjustable boom height, three independently operated boom sections, and a twelve—count 'em, twelve—row width.

The other high-tech machine was a self-propelled hay swather-conditioner. It, too, was a tricycle affair engineered by some machinery masochist because everything on it, from its flapping canvas roller aprons to its impossibly touchy, double-levered steering, was designed to amputate or murder, and sometimes it even slaughtered alfalfa, the lifeblood of our Holstein herd.

That swather, I also remember, was the focal point of the only argument I ever heard between my father and his beloved Uncle Honey, one of our farm's hired hands and the county's most notorious machinery killer.

Early one summer morning while I was milking with Dad, Honey entered the parlor to announce he was going to mow hay with the swather. Calmly but firmly my father told Honey no; the swather, like the combine, was off-limits to Honey's short attention span and even shorter mechanical skills.

The usually quiet Honey, however, persisted; he was going to mow hay with either the new swather or old sickle mower, he repeated.

"No, you're not," my father said sternly. "You absolutely are not going to use the swather and you're not going to use the sickle mower because I'll do it faster and better with the swather."

"Ach," Honey said with Old World disdain, "I bet I can do more with the sickle mower in a morning than you can with that contraption all day."

"I'll take that bet!" my father replied, rising to the challenge of both his management and machinery.

Honey silently waved off his own bet with a firm flick of his hand at my father. He then left, but he did not mow with either machine that day or ever again.

Looking back now, what I heard and saw that morning was an old man's first, only, and doomed-from-start fight over being replaced (displaced, really) in a world literally gearing up to move further faster.

And shortly thereafter, Uncle Honey retired.

> Adults and kids alike worked hard on the farm of my youth. And by worked, I mean really worked—in the fields, in the dairy barn, in the garden. The biggest payoff to all that effort arrived every dinner at noon when we enjoyed the bounty of farm living. I often tell readers and friends if I could recreate one part of my upbringing it would be those gracious, table-bending dinners laden with fresh garden goodness.

I SURVIVED THE GREAT GUEBERT CANNING BATTLE, BARELY

JULY 2, 2000

In his memoir, *Over-fulfilled Expectations*, University of Missouri ag economist Harold Breimyer recalls the advice one Ohio State University extension worker offered a group of Depression-era farmers. "If your wife can't can garden vegetables so they will keep, learn to do it yourself," suggested the extension man.

Had my parents been in that 1930s crowd they would have found the advice redundant. In my youth, they were among America's most competent canners.

In fact, or so it seemed to my four brothers, sister, and me, whatever came into our farm kitchen between June 1 and October 1, be it animal, vegetable, or mineral, was skinned, peeled, cored, or shucked, then blanched, boiled, and cold-packed before being toted to the basement.

During those endless summers, we kids may not have learned how to hit a Little League curveball or do the backstroke, but we did learn that homemade sauerkraut worked well as a paint remover; that field corn, be it DeKalb, Funks, or Pioneer, all tasted the same when it came out of quart jar in December; to never to eat anything labeled "Last of the Garden"; and that botulism was our enemy whereas boiling water was our friend.

The summers of our discontent began each spring on Good Friday when my grandfather arrived with a 100 lb. sack of seed potatoes. Grandpa was not a born gardener; he was a born boss. And, as we soon learned, we kids were born for him to boss.

Grandpa would sit on a bucket under a silver maple and proceed to cut the hundreds of potatoes into thousands of three-eyed seed pieces. We would plant and hill the required ten or twelve quite crooked rows in the huge garden.

When the job was done, Grandpa would rise from his executive bucket and go home, never to inspect our patchy potato planting. I guess he thought he had done his one annual job to ensure his grand-progeny would not starve in the coming winter, thus satisfying his idea of German patriarchal responsibility.

Then my parents would swoop in to plant the vegetables. Five, 300-mile long—at least to us—rows of peas; as many green beans and wax beans; single rows of red beets (yuck), spinach, cucumbers, Swiss chard, pole beans, lettuce, radishes, carrots, broccoli, sweet potatoes, two types of onions, Brussels sprouts (double yuck); and square plots of forty or more cabbages and thirty or so tender tomato plants had (had!) to be planted by nightfall. They always were.

Each seed bore prodigious fruit. Despite an occasional farm drought, we never witnessed a green bean or red beet crop failure. We kids were sentenced each morning to picking bucketfuls of beans or peas, and each afternoon brought the tedious task of podding and ending. Paroles came only when you matured enough to wrestle a hay bale.

And just when the day's heat reached its absolute peak, we began the canning process. Jars. Vegetables. Water. Heat. More jars. More vegetables. More water. More heat.

By dusk, or about the time my father trudged home from the sweaty evening milking and we kids were swimming in the goofy ether of heat exhaustion, we'd eat a cold supper, and if we had been efficient Prussian packers that day, maybe we'd be rewarded with a root beer float before showering and dropping dead into bed to prepare for the next day's great Ball jar battle.

Oftentimes my father and my mother, frustrated that physical threats against our persons were no longer effective tools to ensure our assistance, encouraged us by saying sweetly, "Just think how good it will taste next January."

Certain we'd all be dead by next week from these do-or-die kitchen Kaisers, next January meant nothing to us. Survival mattered and we weren't going to make it.

But survive we did. Thrived, in fact, on all the great-tasting, summer-canned fruits and vegetables.

And now, as summer brings forth another crop from our own gardens, we tell our smarty-pants sons and daughters, "Oh, just think how good it will taste next January."

MORE FISH THAN FIREWORKS AT OUR JULY FOURTH CELEBRATIONS
JULY 4, 2004

One of the first lessons I learned on the 100-cow southern Illinois dairy farm of my youth was that owning cows meant there were just three real holidays a year: Thanksgiving, Christmas, and New Year's.

The only secular exception to that religious regime was the Fourth of July, an all-farm day off, except of course for the dairy barn, for family and hired hands alike. True, Dad helped with the morning milking, but the day's evening milking was done by two of the farm's least cow-impaired laborers.

For a short stretch of the mid-1960s, my parents made the most of the mid-year holiday by hosting the greatest Fourth of July parties a kid on a cow and corn farm twenty miles from town could ever imagine.

The fun began mid-morning when our extended family began to arrive with food, coolers, and lawn furniture. Aunts, uncles, grandmas, grandpas, cousins, and unlinked others often swelled the crowd to near forty by noon.

Great Uncle Honey was the key arrival because he brought the day's essential tool: an exquisitely knotted fish seine. After the men untangled the rolled-up net, aided by laughter and a few eye-opening beers, most everyone walked to the farm's nearby pond to watch the unsteady group gather dinner for the steadily growing crowd.

Honey was in charge. He'd place some of his generation as an anchor on one end of the seine near shore, while Dad and one or two of the younger generation slowly pulled the seine in big, fish-netting loops through the shallow pond's murky water and leg-sucking mud.

When the loops closed, both sets of men struggled like the Lord's Apostles to pull the draught of fishes ashore. Big carp, even bigger buffalo, and hundreds of panfish flopped helplessly in the pasture's tall fescue and dried up cow patties.

Me in my summer farm uniform—bare feet, bare back, and blue jeans—in our backyard about 1965. My sister, Peggy, is in the background and our much better-dressed baby cousin is on the tire swing. It appears we were short on swings and long on inner tubes that year.

We boys, unable to stand the excitement any longer, swooped in to sort the flopping fish. Honey had the final word on fish size and quantity. Small fish went back into the pond while the keepers went into washtubs. Cleaning the fish, and the mud-encrusted seiners, required more laughter and beer than skill and water.

Odd, but I don't remember where we fried the fish. Did Grandpa and the uncles do it in Mom's immaculately scrubbed kitchen (highly unlikely), or was it in the smokehouse with a fryer someone brought? I can't recall.

I do remember that when the fish were ready we all jammed into the kitchen for a pre-meal prayer and an acre of potato salad, fresh coleslaw, the season's first tomatoes, and every kind of red and green Jell-O salad known to Missouri Synod women.

Heaping dinner plates were then taken to assorted card tables and oilcloth-covered butchering tables set in the shade of our backyard's silver maple trees. Chairs were whatever you could find. Kitchen chairs, lawn chairs, benches, upturned buckets.

One July 4th fish fry was filled with tension, however. A young aunt had eloped the week before with a local boy who, despite being a college graduate with a job, was held in low regard by the family. The elopement wasn't nearly as scandalous as the groom's original sin; he was Catholic. The buzz that morning was whether they'd have the nerve to show up.

Oh, they showed up, alright, and in the coolest car I had ever seen: a '49 Merc coupe. And, of course, the family embraced them with backslaps, beer, and Jell-O.

The afternoons of those lazy Fourths passed quickly. The men played loud games of cutthroat Euchre or Pinochle under the trees while the women luxuriated by doing nothing. No canning, no kid-watching, no cooking, no laundry. Supper was leftovers.

At dusk, we all gathered again in the backyard to swat mosquitoes and watch the distant fireworks from Ste. Genevieve, MO, a town across the Mississippi River.

It was a classically American Fourth of July. It was a simple day in a simpler time and it was Thanksgiving, Christmas, and New Year's all rolled into one.

I can't recall the exact genesis of this column but I do recall being angry at some unnamed farm group that had taken me to task for questioning, in print of course, one of its silly dictates to our nation's policymakers in Washington, D.C. Turns out it would be the first of many columns I would write on the subject of farm group silliness and how times have indeed changed.

LESSONS LOST FROM SUMMERS PAST
JULY 17, 1994

On our southern Illinois dairy farm, the third week of July served as a bridge to connect summer's hectic first half to the season's much slower second half.

Then, as now, June and early July were long, endless days melted together with sweat. We cultivated, made hay, cut wheat, baled straw, and milked cows. Mid-July, however, always brought corn tassels, soybean blossoms, the county fair, and, finally, a camping vacation.

But the 100-cow herd still had to be milked. And so, hired men could be left unwatched, like the crops and markets, for a week while our family fished from a rented wooden boat by day and roasted in a giant canvas tent by night.

All of that, of course, occurred a generation ago when late July and August were truly the dog days of Illinois farm life. So little happened in the markets, in Washington, and elsewhere to affect farming that, outside of the cows, the 720-acre farm seemed to glide along on autopilot.

During this slack time, my father helped my mother and us kids can field corn, butcher chickens, make peach butter, dig potatoes, paint outbuildings, and even fold laundry.

Oftentimes he brought the hired men in on big jobs like the one-day, 100-quart peach canning marathon my mother held early each August. Their pay was several quarts each of sweet cling peaches—less if my mother thought they had eaten too many while skinning them—in addition to their regular farm wage. I suspect they would have done it for free because it meant a full day under a shady silver maple.

Although we didn't know it then, my four brothers, sister, and I learned many important lessons during those slow, very domestic weeks. Teamwork, we discovered much later, wasn't a sports concept; it was a family tenet.

Menfolk in the summer kitchen wasn't an ego-busting event, either. It built respect, mostly for my mother and the hard work she did every day. Looking back it is very evident she was as responsible for the farm's success as any of the tanned, well-muscled males who kept those milk checks flowing and the big crops growing.

Of course my parents never explained any of this to us. They didn't have to; they showed us.

Back then we didn't know one farmer who went to Washington to patch cracks, or create them either, in farm programs. Indeed, government was the camel's nose: you kept it outside the tent. You didn't invite it in and you certainly didn't hire some silk-suited jockey to hop on its back and flog it in your special direction.

In fact, I cannot recall my parents ever looking to a farm group or politician for help. When they needed it, they called on friends and neighbors. A pot of coffee and a made-from-scratch cake was the usual solution to most of their mutual woes.

Checkoffs? The only checkoff I remember farmers paying twenty-five years ago was to their church. And when my brothers and I started to earn a wage, fifty cents an hour, we were expected to contribute, also. We did, too, without question.

All of this comes to mind as the quiet season again seeps into Illinois carrying its heat, corn silk, and memories. Those sweet, lesson-filled days seem so far away though. Even more distant is the world that offered such a slow, unchanging pace.

My apron-wearing father in our kitchen, mid-1960s. The farmhouse had no dining room; every meal was shared around our kitchen table. Dad is arranging the seating to enjoy the fish he's just fried for friends and their families. Mom is seated behind our table's one mainstay: cold milk. We boys are licking our chops and preparing to pray. Note the refrigerator magnet's subtle reminder that every recipe could use a bit more . . . something.

Perhaps the fog of subsequent years clouds the memory, but not so long ago there was no such thing as a corn farmer, soybean farmer, dairy farmer, or hog farmer. Back then all were simply farmers. United, one, together.

Someday, quite soon I fear, my generation will look up from our television sets or jet home from Disney World to discover all our money and government programs have crowded out the dignity of honest labor and the self-reliance born of families.

How ironic. We weren't raised that way.

TOUCH MY PEACH TREE?
GO AHEAD, MAKE MY DAY
JULY 22, 2001

The peach tree by my office door is so laden with its fuzzy balls of sun-kissed sweetness that recycled, ¾-inch pipes, wired together teepee style, brace its branches to keep the lovely, nearly-ripe load from breaking 'em. A week from now my chin will be shiny with peach juice.

The pipe trusses weren't needed last July. Early one steamy morning, three adolescent raccoons marched single-file across the yard (the last in line, I swear, shot a "Hey, how-ya-doin!" smirk at me as I drank my coffee on the back porch) and climbed the small tree. Systematically, they then wickedly attacked every nearly-ripe peach.

Horrified by their gluttony, I grabbed a steel rake to roust the bandits. When one of the poachers, perched about eye-level with me, hissed a warning that sounded like "Leave or we'll tear your liver out through your nose," I relinquished any hope of a heavenly harvest.

This year, however, a dog named Maggie, too young to know the difference between a harmless rabbit and a peach-crazed coon, is on patrol. So am I, armed to the liver with a new pellet gun and a nasty attitude.

On the southern Illinois dairy farm of my youth, peaches marked the turning point of summer. When the first peaches arrived every mid-July, the year's hardest work was behind us. The corn was laid-by, the soybeans were in bloom, and golden straw and second-cutting alfalfa were stacked neatly in the barn.

But that first peck of peaches was also the warning shot that the annual day-long peach-canning war under the direction of the greatest peach general ever, my mother, was about to ensue. By dawn's early light of that dreaded day, we foot soldiers were in a local orchard picking up "drops," peaches so ripe they had fallen from the tree. They cost a buck a bushel. By Taps, a sweaty fourteen hours later, 100 or more quarts of newly canned peaches were reposing in the cool cellar.

We had to buy peaches each year because our fruit trees were always too young to bear. They were always too young because Uncle Honey was forever felling the young trees with a clattering sickle mower as he dressed up the fields surrounding our modest orchard. Not until Honey retired did a fruit tree on our farm come of age.

Honey also plugged, or more accurately, plowed under, the farm's only pear tree. The tree stood by itself in a pasture, the lonely sentinel of some long-gone farmstead. Battered by storms and Holsteins, the tree's trunk was so spindly you could see plumb through it. But every year, about silage chopping time, it delivered a couple of hatfuls of golden, pillow-soft pears.

When the pasture fell to the plow and, subsequently, to row crops, the tree fell to Uncle Honey's shiny, five-bottomed spade. The sickly tree toppled and was buried without so much as a hiccup from Honey or the tractor.

That same pasture held one of the farm's loveliest assets: four native pecan trees. The trees were massive—three grown men couldn't reach around any of their gray-brown trunks—and also fruitful. Most Octobers we literally would rake the pecans with our fingers into scoop shovels that we then poured into big gunny sacks to tote home.

One summer day, I came across Uncle Honey's dim-witted son-in-law plunking one of the centuries-old trees with shots from a chrome-plated pistol. Furious at his city-bred arrogance, I took aim and unloaded every invective learned from a decade of hired hands. Tongue-lashed by a foul-mouthed Lutheran lad, he left the farm, and later, Uncle Honey's daughter, never to be seen by me again.

A few years later the Holsteins went into concrete confinement and the pasture went into corn and soybeans. The attendant crop chemicals so weakened the giant trees that all soon fell quickly to weather and disease. In less than a decade, we went from well-provided stewards of those beauties to bottom-line managers who had to beg pecans from neighbors.

I now know we didn't do the right thing.

But I am atoning for my sins. While I cannot grow pecan trees this far north, my yard is a modest forest of peach, pear, apple, ash, maple, birch, and red bud. My trees are me. Touch my trees and you touch my soul.

As such, be you raccoon or royalty, touch my peach tree or any of my trees, and I'll touch you with the working end of a Daisy Powerline Model 880 pellet rifle. Then I'll empty a clip of the most colorful language found this side of hired hand land.

Go ahead, make my day. I'll shoot first and cuss later. And make no mistake, the only way you'll get my peaches is to pry them from my cold, sticky hands.

On October 25, 1994, The Farm and Food File was awarded Column of the Year honors from the American Agricultural Editors' Association (AAEA). The following column is the one judged best by AAEA in its annual competition. I wrote "The View from the Levee" after visiting my parents and brother on a heat-choked Sunday in late July 1993. Although more than 2,000 acres of Indian Farm and neighboring land had been under water by that time, neither my parents nor my brother was dispirited. "The land will be here after the river goes back down," my father noted as we viewed the destruction. "And as long as the land remains, we'll make it." My father's optimism inspired this column, and inspires me still.

THE VIEW FROM THE LEVEE
JULY 25, 1993

When you look east, south, and west from the front porch of my parents' farmhouse, all you see is levee. Strong and silent, the levee guards their 720-acre farm as it curves along the inside shoulder of the confluence of the Kaskaskia and the Mississippi rivers at the midpoint of what topographers call the Great American Bottoms.

Nearly fifty-feet tall, flat-topped, and clad in a coat of waist-deep fescue, the levee has withstood every great flood since its construction in 1952. It held during the then-record flood of 1973 and it holds today, although it now has just two feet of freeboard before it too will be topped.

However, directly across the Mississippi from the farm, the story is sadly different. From atop our levee at night, when it is not raining, we can see Ste. Genevieve, MO, awash in light as sandbaggers toil and sweat to hold off a third record crest in a week.

Just south of Ste. Genevieve, at Kaskaskia Island, the lights no longer fight the night. The historic 15,000-acre island, where the very idea of Illinois bloomed and flourished, lost its second battle in twenty years with the river. When its levee broke in the 1973 flood, the river by our farm dropped two feet in thirty minutes. The Islanders' misfortune became our saving grace. On Thursday, July 22, the island's new levee crumbled, too, but this time the river barely belched before continuing its relentless rise on our levee.

Whenever I go back to the Bottoms, be it during a drought or flood, spring or fall, I either walk or drive the levee to inspect the land, the crops, and the rivers. Each time, I am struck by the irony this levee embodies. Long before man built the levee, the river built the land. Now, to farm the land and build a life, we wall out the builder.

From the levee you can see, and oftentimes feel, the simple beauty and sheer productive power of the Bottoms' famous farmland. Scattered in the distance are a few stately pecan trees and the three unused silos of my father's retired dairy farm.

A mile west is my brother Richard's place, where the old riverbed has left meandering streaks of caramel-colored sand floating amid 1,850 acres of rich, black dirt. Old-timers claim the land that now composes these two farms once supported twenty families, two one-room schoolhouses, and the little village of Moro.

Our farmhouse, the machinery sheds, and heifer barn all emptied and open during the Great Flood of 1993. While the Kaskaskia and Mississippi levees around Indian Farm held strong, constant rain and seep water forced evacuation of everything and everyone in the area. My parents lived for several months in their RV, parked in a neighbor's cattle pasture three miles away. My father took this photo as he surveyed the farm late that summer, just before the Mississippi crested in August.

Now the schools, the village, and the families—save two—are gone, leaving nary a trace they ever existed. Only the land remains.

Indeed, the view from the levee gives you the feeling that only the land in front of you, and maybe the river behind you, will last forever. Even the levee, only a man-made mound, will be breached one day so the river can reclaim what was once naturally hers.

It is this view from the levee that offers the same lesson year after year: this year or last, next year or any future year is quite small—as are we—in the final design already drawn by God. No secrets exist and nothing lies undiscovered that can make our futures any more certain than that of those who came before us. Because of the land, they persevered. So shall we.

Long ago we chose the land. That was wise. Because with or without a levee, only the land lasts forever.

PEOPLE ARE AS IMPORTANT AS THE LAND
JULY 30, 1995

The 720-acre, 100-cow southern Illinois dairy farm of my youth is long gone. Its twelve-foot disks, eighty-horsepower gasoline tractors, and excruciatingly slow six-cow bypass parlor went the way of most things from that era: the smallish iron and its gluttonous appetite for manpower were both easily replaced with bigger iron.

The switch to a power-shifting, front-folding, air-conditioned, globally positioned, computerized agriculture eventually displaced every employee on that farm.

The man who ordered all the replacing, my father, eventually replaced himself. He now is a landlord who cashes steady rent checks instead of a dairy farmer who cashes steadily shrinking milk checks.

Two neighboring brothers, with their huge equipment, cellular telephones, and zero hired labor, now farm the entire spread every year with less muscle and in fewer hours than it took us to put up a single cutting of hay.

I do not miss the sweat, the ninety-hour weeks, or the cows. And I do not begrudge the tenants' ability to do in a month the work that typically took us a year. I do, however, miss the people.

Thirty years ago, our farm was nearly a self-contained village. Three full-time hired men and their families lived on the farm year-round. During the summer, when cultivating, hay making, and straw baling demanded even more brawn, three part-timers were also hired. All earned about $75 a week.

But the full-timers had side benefits: a house, utilities—no telephone, of course—and all the milk they and their families could possibly consume. The meat, sausage, and lard from a two-day, ten-hog butchering every February were divided evenly among them and my family. All shared two fat, open heifers each year, too.

In return for the money, milk, and meat, these workmen with workmanlike names of Howard, Jackie, Charlie, Bobbie, Bill, Bob, and Monroe worked from 6:00 a.m. to 6:00 p.m., six days a week, fifty-one weeks each year. And during their one-week vacation, most stayed on the farm.

The reason they stayed, my brothers and I suspected, was they got more vacation pleasure in endlessly driving past hayfields where we were melting than if they had gone fishing for the week.

While the farm received the benefits of their labor, my brothers and I got something different from these men. They were a rough, uneducated crew who possessed an incredible ability to work, swear, smoke, and drink. Every day, to my mother's often-voiced contempt, these worldly men taught her boys some of life's naughtier pleasures.

At the same time, however, they quietly taught us how to work. And if we failed to follow their hard lead, they mercilessly shamed us back into line by working even harder. We learned more about life, work, and the pure dignity of labor from them than from anyone else.

How my brothers and I repaid them for these important lessons is one of the farm's, and agriculture's, greatest ironies: as we got older, smarter, and stronger, we replaced them.

The choice between them and us was so simple that it wasn't really a choice at all. We could do things they just couldn't, and in truth, weren't trusted, to do: run the combine, plant corn, drive the swather, and take charge of the dairy.

Later, when we slipped into college, our muscles were replaced by round balers, more silos, a bigger combine, 180-horsepower tractors, and a new, efficient milking parlor. We, like them, became obsolete.

What's never obsolete, however, are the lessons these simple, hardworking hired hands taught us. They, more than my father, took the boys of the farm and made them into men.

Thirty years ago the people on that farm were as important as the land. Today, nothing seems as important as the land.

UNCLE HONEY ALL THUMBS

AUGUST 9, 2009

A morning thunderstorm ripped through my rural farmette recently and in its wake I found a front yard peppered with green walnuts, a sky bluer than the Pacific, and memories as warm as the August afternoon that threatened.

On the southern Illinois dairy farm of my youth, everyone—my two older brothers and I, my father, the hired men—spent a minute or two every August day praying for rain. Dad wanted a bountiful harvest; the hired men, Rich, David, and I wanted to avoid baling hay.

Well, at least David and I did, because we were always ready to trade our cows-hay-cows grind for a less sweaty cows-goofing off-cows day. Goofing off on a German Lutheran dairy farm, of course, usually meant lighter work, never actually goofing off.

One such rainy August morning, Dad sent a hired man and Uncle Honey to the farm shop to fix several flat tires that had accumulated.

Knowing the magnificent mayhem Uncle Honey could create, David and I followed because the key ingredients for a perfect storm were about to collide: powerful and potentially dangerous farm tools, an all-too-trusting hired man, and the grand master of farm destruction—our great uncle Honey.

The first tire, a hay wagon one, went well. Honey, after all, could level a mountain with 125 lbs. of air pressure and a big hammer so, after a little cussing by the hired man, the tire seated into the bead of wheel with a loud pop.

Tire two, however, posed a struggle. The trouble was that impatient Honey filled the tube before the hired man had placed it completely in the tire. The tube then pinched, requiring Honey to deflate it and begin anew.

Frustrated, Honey finally ordered the hired man to stick his thumbs between the tire and the rim to prevent the tube from pinching. And, to our astonishment—David and I knew better and we were just kids—the hired man did as told. Honey then re-inflated the tube.

POP! The tire seated and a millisecond later the hired man leapt to his feet with the wheel, tire, and tube dangling from his thumbs.

"My gawd," he screamed when his lungs finally grabbed enough air to vibrate a vocal cord, "ya kilt my thumbs!"

Honey, who never "kilt" anything larger than seven-ounce Budweiser, calmly told the hired man to hold the tire still so he could remove the valve stem core to deflate the tire. As he did, David and I ran.

A moment later, the hired man, cradling his thumbs in a prayerful pose, passed us in a hot trot. A half-minute after that, he drove off in his boat-sized Buick, thumbs upright on the steering wheel. David, Honey, Dad, I, no one really, ever saw him again.

Other rainy August days Dad sometimes gathered Rich and his single-shot .410, David and his single-shot .20 gauge, and me with my single-shot .22, for steamy, silent squirrel hunts in our neighbor's woods.

Since I was the youngest, I often paired up with Dad to tramp the oak and hickory hills in search of acorns and hickory nuts that the squirrels "were cutting on." When we found such signs, we'd lean against a nearby tree to wait for supper.

If a squirrel did appear, the first shot was mine. The .22's clean, little "crack!" was often followed by the bark of Dad's .12 gauge cannon. "We got 'im," Dad would then say. Um, we?

Once, Dad unshouldered his shotgun after its bead fell on a tiny gray squirrel. "More meat on my thumb than that squirrel," he explained.

Of course there was; he had never fixed tires with Honey.

NEITHER CHEAP NOR POOR
AUGUST 12, 2007

Every August, about silage chopping time, my mind flits back to a burning question of my youth: given the old-fashioned way we made corn silage on that southern Illinois dairy farm, were we just poor or were we just cheap?

The best I could figure back then was cheap because the key implements used in the process, the silos and the silage wagons, were homemade.

The silos, in fact, weren't even silos. Instead, three wooden walls created two, 40 ft.-wide by 105 ft.-long above-ground "bunkers" which, because they were above ground level, weren't bunkers either.

They were, however, a testament to simple times and simple materials.

Each 10-ft. wall was constructed of treated (mostly with tar), tongue-and-groove, 2×6s nailed to posts set on 4-ft. centers. The walls, when finished, then served as forms for eight-inch-thick concrete floors that followed.

The silage wagons were equally simple. I clearly remember watching my father and his hired crew building them in the shade of a big maple tree in our yard.

First, they built a strong-backed hay wagon–like frame and floor. The frame, however, featured 8-ft., upright posts that (if memory serves) were bridged side-to-side at the top. The inside walls were planked with pine 1×8s.

The key to the wagons, and what made them nearly self-unloading before anything that inventive had been invented, were the shorter (so silage could be blown over it) front panel and a hinged-at-the-top rear door. Two thick ropes ran the inside length of the wagon from the sliding, front panel to outside the rear door.

When a full wagon arrived at the bunker, stakes holding the rear door were removed and the ropes attached to an idling tractor. The wagon was then pulled forward and, as it moved, the front panel slid backwards to push the silage out the upward swinging back door. When empty, the ropes then pulled the front panel back into position. Slick, eh?

The entire process took just minutes. The idling tractor that held the ropes during unloading was then driven over and over the silage to pack it while awaiting the next load.

As the pile grew, however, so did danger. The packer, usually hired man Jackie, drove the narrow-front tractor up the increasingly steep pile, then, when on top, forward and backwards across the spongy mass that made steering nearly impossible.

Me with a newborn calf, May 1977. The tall wall made up one side of two, above-ground bunker silos we packed corn silage into before any upright silo was built on the farm. We Gueberts rarely had a camera at the ready; my mother-in-law, however, was never without one. Kitty took this photo while visiting the lovely Catherine and me during our year on Indian Farm.

Once, when making the final packing passes of a full bunker, Jackie drove an Oliver 77 over the sidewall. Although nimble was the last adjective anyone ever used to describe the slow-as-molasses man, Jackie instinctively leapt from the machine as it tipped, rolled, and fell upside down several feet to its, and thankfully not his, crushing demise.

I don't know if it was that tractor's fatality, but a couple of years later one of the bunkers was replaced by a 50×24 upright—concrete, aka real—silo. It was sited at the end of the bunker, so the tall walls could shelter the long feed bunk that ran down its center from the silo.

Shortly thereafter I first heard the phrase I quickly came to dread from herdsman Howard upon arrival at the milking parlor to share our before-dawn duty: "Allie Boy, the silage unloader's clogged again."

It was those long, in-the-dark climbs to unclog that cranky unloader, however, that supplied the answer to my annual silage-chopping query. The farm of my youth was operated by people who were neither poor nor cheap.

It was, in fact, operated by geniuses because those bunker silos—without one moving part and still standing strong fifty-five years later—never once needed to be unclogged by anything more than a hungry Holstein.

IT'S AUGUST, TAKE A NAP
AUGUST 12, 2012

One part of every day on the southern Illinois dairy farm of my youth was in-violate: the noon nap. Nearly everyone took one. We didn't rest very long, just thirty minutes or so, because the farm work never rested long. The naps, however, were as integral a part of our farm routine as the big, noon dinners they followed.

Even my great Uncle Honey napped.

Longtime readers remember Honey, my father's uncle. After retirement from a career of grinding the gears on his milk delivery truck in town, Honey made the daily trip to the farm for twenty or so years to, as it turned out, bend, burn, or break nearly everything he touched.

In fact, any silage chopper, pecan tree, sickle mower, plow, field cultivator, rotary mower, barbed-wired fence, hay baler, telephone pole, barn door, parked car, fuel tank, or cow that had the misfortune to be in Honey's path usually left the encounter with a scar, dent, twist, bruise, break, or bandage to mark the occasion.

The great irony to all this iron-bending was that Honey was as mild-mannered as buttermilk. His pulse never topped sixty. Even after he had plowed out the second telephone pole of his short farming career, Honey was as calm as if he had just peeled a potato.

He had the opposite effect on hired men and Holsteins. A simple tractor drive-by or pasture walk-through by Honey caused both to instinctively locate the nearest cover should mayhem ensue.

Fire, too, was a Honey hallmark. Although he never smoked anything, he was never without a little box of strike-anywhere matches that he found cause to strike everywhere. Tree stumps, seed corn bags, straw piles, diesel fuel he poured down ground hog holes, barns—all were touched and torched by Honey and his matches.

Honey was such a firebug that my father often paused during the day just to look around for smoke. Seeing none worried him as much as seeing some. None meant that Honey had either broken an implement or died in the attempt; see-ing some meant that something of ours or the neighbors' (or sometimes both) was likely ablaze.

Despite his gift for destruction, Uncle Honey napped like a baby; a round-tummied, just-fed baby, on the back porch off our kitchen. Since the porch faced north and was screened, neither sun nor bugs interrupted the rest that arrived quickly and settled deeply.

His nap routine was as scripted as a Shakespearean play. After a heaping helping of everything for dinner, Honey would grab the sports section of the *St. Louis Globe-Democrat* and make for the webbed, chaise lounge on the porch.

Once in the chaise, Honey skimmed the sports section's front page, then The Benchwarmer column by the *Globe's* longtime sports editor Bob Burnes. Not long into that reading, however, the paper would begin a slow descent. It might bob upwards once or twice as drifted downward but soon, within a minute or two at the most, it covered Uncle Honey's face and chest like an ink-stained blanket.

Fifteen minutes later, and as noiselessly as he had slipped into slumber, Honey would awaken. After a moment to catch his bearings, he would rise and survey the barnyard as he reached for his straw hat.

Unlike my father, who always removed his work shoes upon entering my mother's kitchen, Honey was never unshod, so he was through the screen door as soon as his hat hit his mostly bald head. It only took a stride or two for him to set a slow course for whatever tractor or implement was being punished by his presence that day.

And everybody, from my father drinking a post-nap cup of coffee in the kitchen, to the sleepy hound under the silver maple tree, would keep a wary eye on him as he did.

THE LAST SUPPER
AUGUST 18, 2013

The weekly newspaper from my hometown brings news that the small, rural Catholic church near the southern Illinois dairy farm of my youth will close its doors next year. A casualty, according to its distant bosses, of too few priests and too many parishes.

It's a judgment day that many of the old timers likely saw coming but few wanted to recognize or plan for. Churches, after all, aren't erected with any thought of closing. Most, in fact, are built on the opposite thought: eternity.

Reading the sad news of St. Leo's fate struck a melancholy chord with its long-ago, one-time neighbor. This old German is gonna' miss that old Vatican City outpost on the bluff.

It's not because the quaint, white clapboard structure overlooking the wide, chocolate-colored Mississippi River bottoms was my family's church; it wasn't. We're stiff-necked heirs of the Great Reformer, Martin Luther.

The church, its parish hall, and rectory, however, were part of the Sunday morning commute to our church, another fifteen miles up the road. That road, St. Leo's Road, was aptly named after the church, its only landmark. Our Sunday drive took us right past its front door each week just as its worshipers were leaving services.

Back then people were quick to leave church but slow to go home. Often neighbors lingered to catch up on whether the hay one had seen the other mow was now in the barn, or if the year's peach crop was going to amount to much. Kids laughed as they ran in the cemetery, and the priest would linger with a flock of perfumed widows on the church's front stoop.

Lately, however, there are few people left visiting, hardly any children to laugh and play, and a priest who must hurry through the chatter to hustle on to his next service an hour later and two towns over.

Those changes doomed St. Leo's and many other country churches in the last few decades. It's a harsh rural reality that church doors close when the Biblical promise of "when two or more are gathered in My name, there I shall be" runs up against too few people and too little money.

It's a law and gospel thing, I reckon. When the Good Book's gospel of eternal life runs into the law of rural economics, temporal defeats biblical most times.

The newspaper article did not relate if the parish would remain the polling place for all local, state, and national elections. Surely parish officials will keep this small service to the community alive because, in fact, there is not one other public building in the whole Brewerville Precinct that could become a substitute.

Whatever its future role might be, families and friends of the old parish are reluctant to let it go.

That reluctance was on full display Saturday, August 3, as the last of more than 100 annual St. Leo's Church Picnics was held on the church grounds. A huge turnout was expected and that expectation was met: more than 1,300 fried chicken dinners, the picnic's second most popular attraction, were served to people who drove from as far as St. Louis, nearly 50 miles to the north, to say goodbye.

After this last supper, most then settled into the evening's main event, bingo, whose most treasured prizes were quilts made by the parish's quilting club.

A week later, the church bulletin served notice that, parish or not, the quilting will continue. "We began quilting downstairs in the Parish Hall last Wednesday, August 7," it announced. "We will meet every Wednesday from 9:00 a.m. to 3:00 p.m. until the end of June 2014."

They won't be alone. Across the county road and next to the church, five generations of St. Leo's faithful lie beneath well-ordered rows of headstones.

These dead will now guard their little, well-loved parish forever.

NOTHING HOTTER THAN AN AUGUST SUNDAY
AUGUST 24, 2008

The only thing hotter than the August nights on the southern Illinois dairy farm of my youth were the August days, and the only thing hotter than the August days were the August Sunday mornings spent wilting in the heat and humidity that St. John's Lutheran Church held so well.

Pastor Gross's stern stare and even more stern sermons added to the communal warmth. When he and his German accent leaned into the Law, you were pretty sure your eternity was going to be even hotter and more endless than any August Sunday morning in church.

To beat the heat, most of the town folk attended the 8:00 a.m. or "early" service. Most of the farm folk, who had cow-milking and other chores to sweat through before church, went to the 10 o'clock service. Since we had cows, we were fixtures of "late" church.

And we always attended; hardy anything kept us home Sunday morning. Not heat, not snow, not flat tires, not sick cows, not corn planting, not nothing.

Oh, there was the very rare Sunday when fate (the devil?) or floodwaters conspired to make attendance impossible. On those Sundays, the entire family gathered in our living room to listen to Missouri Synod services broadcast by radio from Chester, the county seat.

And during those rare (fewer than ten instances in my nearly twenty years on the farm) in-home sessions, we sat as though we were in church. No toys, no books, no goofing off. Our eyes were fixed on the singing, sermonizing radio.

We also listened to "church" on the radio on the back-to-back summer Sundays we traveled to and from our yearly family camping trip. And if a Lutheran service could not be found, a Southern Baptist one would suffice.

Aren't we spiffy in our Sunday finery? Left to right: Richard, me, Peggy, David, and an old-before-his-time Perry. This photo was taken in 1960; our youngest brother, Christian, was still five years into the future.

If we were unlucky and my parents dialed into a Lutheran service after the Baptist one, well, we got a double shot of Good News that trip. What else ya going to do with a carload of questions and camping equipment meandering down some frying pan–hot highway to Lake of the Ozarks or Kentucky Lake?

All the other weeks, however, it was St. John's and heat. Hot Sundays meant even hotter Saturdays because we had to prepare our Sunday best.

First, someone had to iron five, and after my youngest brother Christian was born, six, white shirts. That job fell to either me or my sister.

Next, the car, always the biggest station wagon Detroit could fit between a road's white lines, had to be washed. I don't know why; it just had to. Although I suspected it had more to do with what other Lutherans thought than what the Lord thought.

Then there were shoes to polish and buff. Dad's, Mom's, Richard's, Peggy's, David's, mine, Perry's and, after 1965, Christian's.

Black, white, black, brown, black, black, brown, and white.

Every eight or nine months the shoe owners changed, but the colors and the need for Saturday polishing never did.

About the only cool part of those hot Sunday mornings occurred after the service when many of the now-meek gathered in the shade of the churchyard's trees to talk farming, fishing, or family.

My parents, having spent the previous six days surrounded by cows, corn, and kids, were world-class after-church talkers. Most Sundays, Mom and Dad would be the last yakkers standing in front of St. John's tall steeple. Sometimes they used the serene setting just to talk to each other. Huh.

Alas, those Sundays are long gone. Most churches are air-conditioned today and few parishioners stay around to visit anymore. Too much to do on Sunday.

Almost seems unchristian.

Well, not Lutheran, anyway.

FALL
HARVEST

Fall, of course, meant school, apples, and most importantly, harvest. On Indian Farm, it also meant silage chopping, the World Series, school bus bullies, and clear, cool, starlit nights. Like spring, fall never really descended on southern Illinois; it just crept in on a steady, cow-like pace you hardly noticed. Fall on the farm of my youth was special, and so are my lasting memories of it.

FALL'S COLORFUL AND MEMORABLE CALL
SEPTEMBER 3, 2006

The glowing orange tops of two nearby maples are the first clear announcement that change, despite the day's drilling heat and shirt-soaking humidity, is coming. Their colorful blast is echoed in the growing number of yellowing leaves dancing about my black walnut trees.

It's not yet Labor Day but September can't wait; it's already captured part of August's last week and some of my interest.

I should have seen it coming days earlier when red silage wagons suddenly appeared in a neighbor's farmlot. Silage wagons are a sure sign that September is near.

At least they were on the southern Illinois dairy farm of my youth. Back then, silage chopping arrived in the sun and T-shirt days of mid-August and lasted well into the jacket days of September because our 18×40, 20×70, and 24×60 stave silos had to be stuffed with winter feed.

Each day began the same. Uncle Honey arrived from town at about 7:00 a.m. Hired man Jackie awaited, tractors fueled. Dad had prepared the chopper the night before by changing and "setting" its many razor-sharp, plowshare-sized knives, usually under the farm's sole pole light after the evening milking and his always-late supper.

Every silage-making day was an adventure because Honey, whether standing still or running farm equipment, was always a disastrously destined adventure. Through the years, though, he never killed or disabled anyone.

The same can't be said for most of our silage equipment. Honey killed one silo blower in the early 1970s and seriously maimed a silage wagon (or two) every year.

My brothers and I were part of the silage corps; we ran wagons between Honey and Jackie. The farm had three silage wagons: one being filled by Honey; one being emptied by Jackie; and one on the road, either full or empty, between the two.

We boys had to hustle to keep up with the two men at either end of the feed chain—especially Honey, who did everything one gear too fast and with one eye too few on his co-workers. Jackie, naturally, did most things a gear too slow and with his rheumy blue eyes wide open, often on Honey.

Honey's speed, combined with his acute machinery attention deficit disorder, promised two events every silage season.

The first was a pathological over-filling of the wagons. If the wagon held ten tons, Honey would pour on twelve. If he got twelve on the last one, he'd aim for thirteen on the next one. Then fourteen. It was an annual "Honey, I Shrunk the Wagons" game.

And the wagons always lost. Busted tie rods, bent running gears, and blown tires were part of every silage season on the farm. Some days Honey delivered all three to the same wagon either in series or, quite miraculously, simultaneously.

The second inevitability was Honey's complete disregard for my brothers and me when we exchanged wagons. The routine was simple and never varied.

It began when Honey finally looked back to note he had again overfilled a wagon. He'd stop briefly to pull a rope that looped from his tractor seat to the chopper's spout, then down to the trailing wagon's hitch pin to unhook the groaning wagon. We then would swing in behind Honey's rig to deliver the empty.

We waited, however, until he had pulled ahead, chopping silage onto the ground the whole way, to give us the necessary space to pull in front of the full wagon. We'd unhitch our empty, pull to the side, dismount, and walk over to the chopper to hook the empty to Honey's rig.

No sooner had we dropped the hitch pin to reform his silage-chopping train, Honey would slam that big Oliver into a forward gear—he hadn't throttled back or disengaged the chopper during the exchange—to roll on and send a stream of freshly chopped silage bullets on us at the speed of light. He was an uncanny marksman with the chopper; he never missed.

It was never intentional; Honey simply never looked back. Honey, as I've reported here before, never looked back and never stopped.

I, however, often look back, and when I do, I usually find my wonderful Uncle Honey always looking straight ahead.

COLOR SUMMER'S END YELLOW

SEPTEMBER 4, 2005

The end of central Illinois' heat-stoked, rain-starved summer is whispered in the yellow leaves rattling on my backyard's black walnut trees. September's first cool breeze shakes some loose and the faded leaves slowly settle on the browning lawn.

Soybean leaves, too, are yellowing. Many, though, sapped of water and nutrients by wave after wave of heat-fueled mites and aphids in August, are already gone. Acre-sized blotches of dead plants float amid lime green seas of beans the bugs bypassed.

The corn is dead maize stalking, bushwhacked by June's lack of rain and July's murderous heat. Farmers hope for 100 to 130 bushels, half of last year's remarkable yields. Maybe they're right; September's yellow will tell the tale.

The cash grain markets long ago yellowed. Corn futures drift fifty cents per bushel under July's highs and bean futures sag a wallet-cracking buck-and-a-half under mid-summer's high water mark.

And now, the most certain sign of summer's leaking away—big, yellow school buses—lumber to a stop and lumber to a start up and down the crop-lined roads. The machines appear far too big to carry the handful of children that remain in the country.

That wasn't so forty years ago. The bus I rode for twelve years was a rolling sardine can jammed with kids aged six to seventeen. We rode it for an hour in the morning and an hour in the afternoon because we had to.

"The bus stops at the mailbox twice a day," we were told if we griped about the brain-frying ride; "I suggest you get on it or you walk." Since we lived eighteen miles from school, the admonition was more like a sentence than a suggestion.

We weren't the only farm kids with flinty, public transportation–supporting parents. Nearly every rural elementary and high school-aged son or daughter who lived more than a mile outside of town had parents cut from the same cloth.

Some of us spent the long, often dusty rides fruitfully: reading books, doing homework, or planning 4-H meetings. Others, usually the less scholastically inclined, filled their boring breech with card games, saucy stories, and bullying anyone within arm's reach.

The bullies weren't the likable Eddie Haskell-types. They were tough and mean and not afraid of your blood or theirs. Once I saw one pull a shiny switch-blade knife on another and I also saw in the guy's yellowed, bared teeth and hooded green eyes that he would use it.

I don't know what the drivers were paid for their duties, but on our bus route, the longest in the school district if not the history of the nation, it could not have been enough given the yelling, swearing, and mayhem that rode with them.

Our route went through drivers faster than the drivers went through clutches. Few men, there were no women drivers back then, wanted the rock road run to the River Bottoms. Only one, the quiet, reed-thin Ralph, lasted longer than a year.

Ralph succeeded where others either failed or went mad because of a clever trick he employed whenever his havoc meter redlined: he simply pulled off the road, switched off the bus's ignition, and, calm as a napping cat, wordlessly leaned back into his vinyl seat until we morons noticed we weren't moving.

The first time Ralph pulled the pull-off-the-road trick, the back-of-the-bus bullies pelted him with screams and curses. Ralph's reply forever destroyed their never-before challenged power. He pulled, again wordlessly, the key out of the ignition and slipped it into his pocket.

In two minutes the bus was as quiet as a cemetery on a winter's night. Two minutes of silence after that, Ralph re-fired the engine and we proceeded homeward.

The lesson was quick and indelible. In the subsequent two or three years he drove the route, all Ralph had to do was downshift a gear along a spot in the road where no one on the bus lived and everyone's lips locked tighter than a rusty lug nut on an old hay wagon.

Ah, September, you're yellowing yet still wonderfully alive.

I wrote the following column the day after Mary Grace's wedding ceremony to Andrew Foxwell in a hot, green garden in Washington, D.C. It didn't take long to write; I had been planning it longer than Gracie and Andrew had been planning their wedding, which was indeed only a few short months. I finished editing the column at 5:00 a.m. two days later in a hotel room in Kentucky, and later that morning, the lovely Catherine and I drove to Lanes Landing Farm for a memorable visit with our friends Tanya and Wendell Berry. The four of us shared stories of our children growing, eagerly flying away, and thankfully, later flying back home to the farm—and back to us.

DAY OF DAYS
SEPTEMBER 9, 2012

Someone—my great grandfather, my grandmother, my dad, someone—told me how fathers announced the wedding of their daughters more than a century ago in the small, southern Illinois farming community where I was raised.

The story goes like this: after a wedding date was set, the bride's father saddled his finest horse to ride throughout the neighborhood carrying a cane covered in ribbon bows. When he arrived at the home of someone to be invited to the wedding, he'd slip a bow from the cane and hand it to the family as the official invitation.

Sometimes, the story continued, the father's good news was met with so much good cheer that only the horse was clearheaded enough to find the way back home.

Whoever told me the story, its original source likely was my great grandfather, a blacksmith in the little town. He loved stories and this one is nearly as lovely as any bride.

My parents' wedding, September 2, 1950, in that same town, was to be a garden affair. After the Lutheran ceremony, everyone was invited to the edge of town where my mother's family home and sprawling lawn was the reception site.

The planning and preparations had been meticulous. Chickens, from the farm my mother and father had already established, had given their short, plump lives for the main entrée. Potatoes, peas, and pies also lay waiting the final "Amen."

Then the rain began to fall. And fall and fall.

On short notice, everything—bride, groom, chicken, guests, minister, pies, and laughter—were driven between raindrops in my Uncle Honey's milk delivery truck to the Lutheran school for a dry reception. The day hadn't turned out as planned, but no one who attended ever forgot it.

Weddings of my brothers and sister, all joyous, hold similar memories. For example, my oldest brother's wedding was held on the evening of the hottest March Saturday in anyone's memory. The church, the same one my parents had been married in a generation before, was a stained glass steam bath; its air hot, stale, and unmoving.

Soon, however, other things, much bigger things, began to move. The first was a cousin, standing up stiff-legged for my brother. After two steps backwards, Danny fainted with great drama, he went down in a crashing heap like a boxer whose lights just got punched out.

Our Mary's day of days, September 2, 2012. Left to right: me, Gracie, Andrew, the lovely Catherine, and Lt. Paul in his Navy dress blues. Andrew brings many wonderful gifts to our family including, thankfully, the height gene.

The next to go was my sister; she simply melted into a perfect puddle of taffeta and teased hair.

When others began to wobble and my brother and not-yet-sister-in-law still a prayer and a hymn away from "I do," Pastor Holstein (really, I'm not making this up) paused to survey the carnage. It was bad; two down, two looking pretty pasty, and the rest sweating like a hay crew.

Pastor then raced through the vows; I never heard "I pronounce you husband and wife" and I was fifteen feet from him. He mumbled a blessing and that was that.

This September 2nd was equally hot and steamy in Washington, D.C. Rain-heavy clouds kept the day dressed in gray and sprinkles slickened the bustling streets in the middle of the afternoon.

At 5 o'clock, however, a strong sun defeated the day's dullness and our Mary Grace, daughter of the lovely Catherine and me, slowly walked through a leafy Georgetown garden to wed Andrew Foxwell, one of Wisconsin's finest sons, before forty-five friends, family, and God.

Unlike my parents' wedding sixty-two years earlier to the day, no rain fell and, unlike my brother's wedding, no one wearing a pressed suit coat or tall hair wilted in the heat. It was, as Wendell Berry wrote lovingly in a poem to celebrate his daughter Mary's wedding in January 1981, our "Mary's Day of Days," and it was wonderful.

Hey, give us three generations and we'll get most anything right.

REMEMBER HONEY?
SEPTEMBER 15, 2002

The slightest, vaguest passing thought often ignites the mind, and in a nanosecond it's moving at warp speed to the land of lovely lost thoughts.

During a daydream recently, I pondered why my backyard pear tree is barren this year. Before my brain found the answer, an errant spark lit a dark corner of my memory to spotlight the lonely pear tree on the farm of my youth. The weathered tree, the only remnant of long-gone farmstead, stood ready to deliver, as it did each September, a hatful of golden pears.

Then, without touching the remote control, my brain replayed the video of that lovely tree's ugly demise. My Uncle Honey simply plowed it under with a roaring 1850 Oliver and five-bottom IH plow.

Longtime readers of this column may recall Honey and recognize from the pear tree incident the main ingredients of a classic Honey hit. For the uninitiated or merely forgetful, that recipe includes:

- One tractor at full-throttle connected to either a plow, rear-mounted cultivator, silage chopper, sickle mower, or disk. A V-8, 1968 Pontiac Catalina all by itself worked well, too.
- Any field or road near a telephone pole, barn, fence, tree, or river.
- Add Honey and wait, usually only minutes, for the sound of a splash, a crashing tree, crushing metal, snapping wood, or any combination thereof.

For all the noise and mayhem he created, Honey, as his childhood nickname implied, was pathologically pleasant. He loved the St. Louis Cardinals, his daily, seven-ounce Budweiser, and silence.

He was pleasantly pathological, also. Imperturbable, Honey quietly took everything life brought him—his milk delivery trucks before retirement, my father's farm machinery after retirement—and methodically wrecked it.

It was one of our family's deepest mysteries. On his feet, Honey was quiet, kind, and generous. On a tractor seat, he murdered everything animate or inanimate. If Honey was astride or beside farm machinery, mayhem was a moment away. He lacked only two things for complete happiness: safety and enough shear bolts.

I once witnessed Honey inadvertently plow a deep furrow with a pull-type silage chopper. Later I saw him accidentally chop silage with a semi-mounted plow. He regularly mowed down fences with disks, sickle mowers, and cars, but I never saw him actually mow one fencerow.

Cattle feared him; dogs loved him.

The only cross words my father ever came close to speaking to his quiet uncle was the time Honey asked for the chainsaw.

He carried a pocketful of unshelled peanuts everywhere; my father, trailing in Honey's twisted metal wake, carried aspirin. His pocket also held a two-inch bolt, the perfect length to prop open the handle of the diesel fuel hose. That meant the barnyard periodically flooded with diesel.

Honey believed a man wasn't a man if he didn't carry matches. Smoke became our way of finding him on the farm. If it was white and gone in five minutes we were relieved because we knew he hadn't wrecked anything—yet.

Matches and five gallons of diesel were Honey's groundhog eradication program. The two also served as his Johnson grass and tree stump removal programs. Since Johnson grass, tree stumps, and groundhogs were the farm's principle crops for years, Honey never went to the field without his trusty pyrotechnic twins.

Rural fire districts? They were invented because of Honey.

As were safety glass, safety glasses, safety shields, life jackets, jaws-of-life, EMTs, SUVs, ABS, hard hats, and steel-toed boots.

The national seatbelt law wasn't because of Ralph Nader; it was because of Honey. Tractor roll cages? Honey must have had a hand in that, too.

And now as the yellows of September once again checker the fields of autumn, I see Honey killing our pear tree again. We loved that tree and we loved our kind, killer Honey. Loved him to death.

We just kept our distance when he was operating farm machinery because we didn't want to die with him.

LOOK TO THE STARS
SEPTEMBER 16, 2001

Very late the night before the horror in New York, I stood in the enveloping darkness at the end of my driveway to look skyward at the spectacular, silent stars. One of the many benefits of living in a small Midwestern farm town is that you can stand in the middle of the street day or night as long as you wish, or until you feel foolish, without causing one local eyebrow to raise.

But before my television-lit eyes adjusted to the dark that night, other senses took over. A powerful, palpable stillness filled the cool night. A long-gone hired hand of my youth often described that kind of dead calm as "not enough wind to rattle a maple leaf."

No sooner had that phrase hit my brain did the small man's leathery face, complete with its ever-present, three-day-stubble, emerge from the closet of my memory. I grinned.

Jackie was a world-class complainer who complained so much and so often about everything, that when he complained about the lack of wind, my family's only reply was always a grin.

The pleasantness of that rediscovered face was broken by the sweet, low call of a barn owl eyeing me from atop a tall spruce across the street. When his rhythmic call ended, a second owl replied from the distance. The hoot-hooting became a near-chatter as they exchanged breaking news. He's standing in the street. In the street? Now he's looking up. At you? Yes, but he appears harmless. Harmless? Yep, and lost.

Kind of. Lost in thought as I began to sort through the blended smells of the deep night. There were hints of fresh grass and wood smoke, leftovers from the neighbor's evening chores. Next came a whiff of corn dust, sent by the early harvesters of our spotty, weakened crop.

The earthy scent pushed my mind back to the harvest of 1967 when, with an Oliver 77 and 100-bushel, self-unloading wagon, I slowly trailed my father's dust-spitting IH 303 combine as he shelled corn. My job was to haul corn from him to the bin. In fact, it was secondary to the really important work of the day: holding a transistor radio to my ear as I listened to the St. Louis Cardinals play the Boston Red Sox in the World Series.

As I stood in the street, I clearly saw my father's corn-dust covered face crack´ into a smile as I loudly shouted game updates each time he stopped the lumbering machine to empty its overflowing grain tank into the wagon.

Dear Lord, I whispered to no one but the silent night and the gossiping owls, thank you.

Then I looked up at the stars, the million, brilliant, stunning stars. A month ago, while fishing in the quiet woods of Canada, my farm town friends and I laid outside in the midnight darkness to marvel at the almost reachable stars. In the first minute of the first night of looking we were rewarded with two streaking, burning stars blistering the black sky.

No wows during that Monday night's stargazing, though. Only quiet, eerie dots of million-year-old light now igniting other thoughts. I said a prayer, this one for a farmer friend's mother who had passed the night before. As I finished, the twinkling stars whispered "All is peaceful now."

I followed a weak path of starlight toward the North Star. Before I found it, however, my eyes moved to a faint light dribbling from the upstairs window of my bedroom. A tiny, twenty-watt bedside reading lamp was still at work even though my lovely bride had long before fallen asleep. The dim rays beckoned me like a lighthouse to her safe, calm harbor.

Lingering but a moment more, I looked and looked again at the everlasting stars as I said my evening prayers to the everlasting God.

And the love and the hope I felt at that moment combined to dispel any chill of that late night, or of an unknown future.

I grew up on a farm filled with hired men. Tall or short, shaven or whiskered, educated or ignorant, most hired men came and went like seasons—uneventfully. Faces in the manly crew changed often and, sometimes, overnight. A few remained for months, and only a couple stayed on for years. None should be forgotten. One certainly won't: Jackie.

THE LIFE AND TIMES OF ONE WORKING MAN
SEPTEMBER 21, 1997

On a recent early morning drive to a noontime appointment a state away, my drowsy eyes spied the telltale short shanks of a corn field recently cut down by a silage chopper.

The 65-mph glimpse tripped many thirty-year-old memories about September silage chopping on the southern Illinois dairy farm of my youth. I could hear the throaty roar of spinning chopper knives. For a moment, I saw tanned men on green tractors pulling red silage wagons beside gray silos.

As these vignettes spun into a longer playing daydream, I clearly saw Jackie—a hired man who came with the farm when my grandfather purchased it in the late 1940s. That's the way it was in the Mississippi Bottoms back then; like a barn or a fence, people often came with the land.

And Jackie did because, in truth, he had no choice. He was an ageless bachelor who needed the job to support his mother and three brothers. And since he could neither read nor write, his destiny was that of a farmhand. He was the runt of the clan, five-foot-six and no more than 140 pounds when he still had all his teeth.

For years, Jackie had but two uniforms, a summer one and a winter one, and neither landed in a washing machine more than once a week. His summer attire was two socks, two work shoes, one colored T-shirt, and a pair of stiff Duck Head overalls. His winter outfit was the same but it included long underwear, Duck Head coveralls, and a cap with earmuffs.

Jackie's daily schedule varied as little as his clothes. He'd arrive at the dairy barn at six each morning for a cup of Folgers instant coffee and the day's marching orders from my father. He'd then work 'til noon, go home to check his mail and grab lunch, then return to work until six o'clock Monday through Saturday, fifty-one weeks a year. His unchanging days melted into unchanging weeks into unchanging years.

Usually, the highlight of Jackie's day was the mail. It was his link to the outside world; his family never owned a television or telephone. Since he couldn't read, one of my brothers or I would read his mail to him before the long afternoon of work began at 1:00 p.m.

Jackie could work, too; he was a tough little man. His standard jobs bordered on the mechanical: stacking hay, hauling grain, spreading manure. He never milked the cows, drove the combine, cultivated, or mowed hay because, as he made plain, he just didn't want to.

Jackie never made what today would be called a living wage; nobody on that farm did. But since his job included a free house, utilities, meat, and milk, Jackie's shiny leather billfold, carried in the bib of his overalls, always contained what he called his "walkin' around" money.

And if he wanted a new shotgun or a new car, he'd just go to the bank to withdraw the necessary cash from a rarely tapped savings account. Because he couldn't write, he did not maintain a checking account.

One Sunday evening while milking with his brother Howard, I was told the story of how Jackie remained illiterate even though his siblings "got schoolin.'"

According to Howard, Jackie was in the second grade of the nearby one-room schoolhouse when Santa came to visit one bleak Depression Christmas. Jackie, a sharp-eyed kid, thought St. Nick looked like the neighborhood poacher everybody knew only as Buck.

"So's when Jackie got on Santa's lap to get his candy," related Howard, "he yanked off the whiskers that old Buck was wearing to show everybody that Santa was a fake. The schoolteacher took him outside and blistered him with a pecan branch. Then she sent him home without his candy. After that, he never went back. Yessir, that's how it was."

Howard told the tale with humor, laughing as his mind replayed the scene of fat, old Buck being unmasked by scrawny, little Jackie.

Jackie lived the next fifty years within a half mile of that schoolhouse, working thirty of those years on our farm until, don't you know it, some smarty-pants college kid came back to the farm and replaced him.

Two years after I pushed him out of his near-lifetime job, I left the farm for college again. By then, however, Jackie had a job stacking boxes at a nearby cake mix factory. Cancer claimed him a decade later, a shriveled, still-tanned runt of a quiet, working man.

A generation ago, there were a million or more Jackies in American agriculture. Few, if any, had any stories written about their plain, honest lives.

Now one has.

ROADS TAKEN
OCTOBER 2, 2011

The usual six-mile drive home from Sunday church took a pleasant turn some weeks ago. As I headed back to the farmette for more coffee and more newspapers, my mind went a different way and, without one turn of any wheel, I was on my way to the southern Illinois dairy farm of my youth.

Back then most Sunday drives home from church featured three elements: a well-scrubbed Ford station wagon with at least five kids and no seatbelts in its back seat, the car radio relaying the tape-recorded highlights of the St. Louis Cardinals' past week, and the penetrating smell of my father's slow-burning Camel cigarette.

And if it was summer, all the windows of the big-fendered boat would be down so we could enjoy what was sure to be the closest thing to air conditioning we'd feel all week.

Winter delivered the opposite. Windows tightly closed so the rolling oven would, we vainly hoped, roast us well-done so we'd remain warm for the next seven days.

And spring, summer, fall, or winter, we boys—Rich, David, me, and Perry— sat like straight-backed little sinners all in a row, felt hats atop no-smile faces made stiff by starched collars, narrow ties, and real fear of an angry God.

Or so it seemed. Back then the pre-war Lutherans, pre-World War I that is, were long on Law and short on Love. When a young minister arrived in the mid-1960s and began to teach the New Testament as much as the Old, mild grumbles about too-little Law and too-much Gospel filtered through after-service visits in the churchyard.

My parents, to their eternal credit, never passed on the gripes. They found little fault in their new shepherd's preaching and no fault whatsoever in his perfect, dairy-country name: Pastor Holstein.

In the 100 or so drives to and from church each year, the after-church drives during the fall were best.

In almost half of those 1960s Septembers and Octobers, the Cardinals were either fighting for a pennant or a World Series ring. That made the Sunday radio replays like a victory lap; we already knew how they ended so we'd cheer before Jack Buck or Harry Caray joyously announced a Bob Gibson strikeout or a Lou Brock stolen base.

We loved those teams. Still do.

A curious little irony of the drive home, however, was that we Lutherans spent most of it on St. Leo's Road, a meandering blacktop named after a middle-of-nowhere Catholic church that commanded the high bluffs overlooking our farm.

St. Leo's, its rectory, social hall, empty one-room school, and small burying ground seemed both misplaced and perfectly placed. Misplaced because few farms and fewer people were nearby; well-placed because from the shade of its broad maples you could see the confluence of the Kaskaskia River with the Mississippi miles away.

A second lovely irony each week was that on our way to church we usually chugged by just as the "Papists" were letting out. That meant we had to toss a weak wave or smile at our oh-so-heathen neighbors while my father would smile and acknowledge the menfolk through his open window. (Never mind that I would later marry one of their Roman sisters, the lovely Catherine.)

We'd slowly putter through, then head for the Lutheran bastion farther up the road and, hopefully, way, way up the road: heaven. Three hours later, heaven and hell were left behind and eighteen or so miles to home beckoned.

Recently, it beckoned again. Maybe it was the crackling blue sky that morning, or maybe it was the smell of harvest, thin and drought-starved though it is this fall.

Or maybe it was just a graying farmboy, having just heard the Word, looking homeward.

OH, WE KNEW COLD
OCTOBER 4, 2009

The distant hickory trees sport golden crowns and the neighbor's white oak has begun to flash hints of scarlet when the wind rustles its leaves. The slow, colorful drift into winter has begun; the wheels of nature are turning.

The wheels of harvest, however, are not. September is gone but nearly every acre of still-green corn and finally yellowing soybeans in my central Illinois neighborhood remains. As farmers impatiently wait, most speak of a "long" and "cold" harvest.

No doubt, yet this year's slow-to-start endgame will be shorter and warmer than any harvest my family experienced in the twenty-five or so years I was on our southern Illinois farm. Every harvest back then, from the mid-1950s through the late 1970s, was an endurance race that featured more endurance than racing.

To hear my father recall, his first harvest—1951—had to be his worst. Endless rain, snow, and mud slowed that year's corn picking to a horse-drawn crawl as he used a team of horses to bring in the crop by hand, fifty or so bushels at a crack.

By the time he was done late that winter, he joked, he had spent more time with those horses than with his young bride, my mother. In the way he spoke of his team, I often suspected he regarded 'em almost as much.

After my parents moved from their hardscrabble hill farm to a huge-by-comparison, river bottom farm near the Mississippi, a two-row mechanical picker replaced Dad's two hands and two horses.

I don't remember ever seeing that picker picking, but I do remember seeing it restfully rust in the back of the barn. It was finally sold sometime in the mid-1960s when, I guess, Dad and Grandpa thought the new, little Massey combine that had retired it might be a keeper.

And it was, but what a yapping toy poodle it was (I think a Massey-Harris 35), compared to today's ravenous wolves. It rattled and whirred with unguarded belts, chains, and augers to deliver a dribble of shelled corn into a thirty-five-bushel grain hopper.

And it had a viciously temperate heart because the operator, only my father, sat in the open air almost directly over the header. That meant he ate bugs and dirt during wheat harvest, and snow and dirt during corn harvest.

Snow seemed always on the menu during corn harvest. Maybe it was because back then, no one finished planting corn until late May. Maybe it was because

Part of the dairy complex about 400 yards south of our farmhouse. This photo was taken in the early 1970s as a promotional piece for White Star Silo Company, then of Ste. Genevieve, MO. White Star Silo Company is still in business; it is now located in the wonderfully named burg of Germantown, IL.

our 100 milk cows limited the time Dad could combine. Then again, maybe it was because we were just slow.

The little Massey was replaced by an IH 303 combine. While bigger, the operator still sat, or, as my father often did out of boredom, stood, smack in the middle of all the dirt, bugs, and weather.

One fall harvest, however, was so long and so cold that Dad baling-wired several storm windows together to form a three-sided, open-topped cab on the 303 to at least cut the wind. While it worked reasonably well, it looked as though the Beverly Hillbillies, and their combine, were our partners that fall.

Then, in the late 1960s or perhaps it was 1970, Dad bought the last combine he'd ever drive, a crossbred White-Oliver. The companies had recently merged so the combine was painted Oliver green and the three-row (count 'em!) corn head was Cockshutt red.

It matched the season perfectly when we picked corn every Christmas thereafter.

More importantly, it sported a heated and every-now-and-then air-conditioned cab. Little wonder Dad kept that relic running nearly into the twenty-first century; both he and Mom were warm. He in his combine and Mom with all her storm windows.

FALLING
OCTOBER 7, 2012

Apparently a notice went out a week ago to all the Illinois blue jays that the acorns on a shingle oak outside my office were ripe for the picking. Within hours, a dozen or more jays appeared in the tree's top branches to pluck, shuck, and consume the soft fruit of the slick-leafed tree.

Now, four or five days after the blue jay Woodstock began, the ground under the tree is a carpet of acorn hulls and caps that crunch, with an almost delicious snap, beneath my steps to and from the mailbox.

That's what fall sounds like this year. Snap. Crackle. Squawk.

The jays didn't come alone. Fat-cheeked ground squirrels, feasting on the nutty debris field, arrived a day thereafter. A month ago, nary a one showed its buck-toothed face. Today they must be texting and Tweeting to every brother, sister, and cousin to come share the fat times because the squeaking varmints dash and dart everywhere.

Old Maggie, the farmette dog, cares little about the critters that threaten the rule of her mild kingdom. Age and aches take her slowly from one sunny part of the yard to another for long, hard naps in the autumn's just warm-enough sun. Increasing deafness promotes her slumber, too; the less she hears the more she dreams.

Most late afternoons, however, Maggie is rested enough for a walk in the woods. Like other seniors in the neighborhood, though, the sinking sun calls her home to where warmth, supper, and more sleep await.

On warm days, an open back door brings the sounds of another corn and soybean harvest. At night the steady whine of grain dryers provide a one-note symphony that crickets and owls occasionally harmonize to. Later, a rising, weak moon provides a silky glow to the unerring concert.

Few predicted a colorful fall this year, yet the maples, hickories, and ash are awfully showy for all the heat and dryness they endured this spring and summer.

They turned yellow, red, gold, and plum earlier than in past years and will, I reckon, become bare-branched earlier, too.

That's fair. April arrived in March, so if November arrives in October then some sort of seasonal balance will be restored.

Today's damp, cool morning turns my attention to the winter's woodpile. A long wall of aged, split red oak (too good, really, to burn in the fall) stands ready, a one-minute wheelbarrow ride from the downstairs stove.

Nearby, another long, deep stack of oak, elm, and hickory sits under roof as it awaits its hot fate in the upstairs stove. It is dry and beautiful and I can smell the hickory as I walk past the small, open-faced shed.

That wonderful aroma takes me homeward, and fifty years backwards, to the same thoughts I had as a child on the early morning bus rides to school.

That bus, before books filled the hour-long ride a few years later, was a magic carpet that carried me through hills and hollows and towns and fields I'd never yet seen, and every day I was absolutely thrilled to climb aboard to see it all again.

Fall mornings, like this morning, were the absolute best to be on that bus because the sights and smells—steam-breathing cattle casually chewing as we lurched by, barnyard chickens scattering as children raced to catch us, dew-draped corn pickers waiting to go back to work, beat-up pick-ups at the end of dusty lanes packed with sulky teenagers, a whiff of burning coal—were almost too much for a young boy to take in.

Today, however, they're just enough to make an aging observer smile as another year's leaves drift on a gentle breeze toward an aging, resting dog who dreams not of corn yields or needed rain or national politics. She just rests in the beauty of another glorious fall day.

Smartest dog I ever did see.

A SEASON OF HOPE
OCTOBER 10, 2004

The words "Fall Classic" meant nothing to me on the southern Illinois dairy farm of my youth; that is, until 1964. That year, after eighteen years of futility, the St. Louis Cardinals won the National League pennant on the final Sunday of the season.

Like all life-changing events, I know exactly where I was when beer-cheered Cardinal announcer Harry Caray began his mad "Cardinals win the pennant!"

chant. I was dancing in the dairy barn with my oldest brother Rich as he and a hired man were about to begin the evening milking.

I also recall where Dad was; he was doing what he did every day every October, November, and most of December: eating corn dust atop a tiny, two-row IH 303 combine. And Uncle Honey, the only one in the family who could match my Cardinal zeal, was plowing near (likely, too near) the dairy barn.

I ran to report the greatest news of my life to Honey. From 100 yards, however, my very wonderful, very reserved great uncle saw it easily in my wide smile, and he and that Case 930 never broke stride. He just nodded, tossed me an acknowledging grin, and continued to turn black slabs of southern Illinois toward the sun.

Like Honey, my fourth grade teacher, the widely feared Mrs. Myers, was a rabid Redbird fan. The only other real passion she possessed, I reckoned, was beating schoolboys with a paddle cut from a bed slat. (Classmate Ricky Wetzel was the first to discover Mrs. Myers was a right-handed power-hitter. I was the second.)

But Mrs. Myers turned into a quivering lump of Cardinal red Jell-O for one glorious week in 1964. She snuck a radio into our classroom during the Series so we could listen. She even drew a baseball field on the chalkboard to track who was playing where, which player was at bat, what the batter's count was, and who was on deck. My love of learning subsequently spiked that week spent in her class.

My other indelible memory of the '64 Series came during Game Four, a Sunday match-up at Yankee Stadium. For some forgotten reason, we didn't pick corn that day but stayed in town after church for dinner at my father's grandparents.

I loved visiting my great grandparents because Grandpa's backyard barn held a fabulous playroom, his old blacksmith shop. Yet I wanted to go home that day because I knew if we stayed, I'd have to watch the game on a television with a picture snowier than a Canadian winter.

But we stayed and I saw a shadowy Ken Boyer hit a grand slam home run to win the game 4–3 and tie the Series. I was flying so high afterwards that another grandpa, Dad's dad, ordered me outside so the grown-ups could play Pinochle.

The injustice of it still stings. They could get rowdy with their cards but I couldn't get rowdy with my Cards?

Three years later, Grandpa Guebert, a stockbroker, made amends. While attending some big shot meeting in late 1967, he asked Boston Red Sox star Carl Yastrzemski, a guest speaker, to personalize and autograph a baseball for me.

The great prize was made all the greater because my Cardinals had beaten the Red Sox in a seven-game World Series a couple of months before. That ball, signed to Allan Guebert and not Alan Guebert, rests on a shelf just a few feet from my desk today. The autograph is fading but the warm hug Grandpa gave me with the ball will never fade.

Like forty years ago, this October finds the Cardinals reaching for another World Series. It also finds America again in the middle of a brutal, ugly war, a nation-dividing presidential campaign, and another bountiful harvest.

But it's not 1964. My youth is long spent and Uncle Honey has long passed. Hardly anyone plows anymore and no one picks corn with an IH 303.

Gone too are the giants, a farmboy's heroes—100,000 cows and a half-million corn rows away from the big leagues of anything. I loved them all and I miss them all.

Mostly, though, I miss what October used to bring: a season of hope.

CARPENTER, I AM NOT
OCTOBER 30, 2011

Some serious outdoor carpentry this fall quickly proved, again, the enormous amount of woodworking skills I failed to acquire on the southern Illinois dairy farm of my youth.

It's easy to peg the origins of this deficiency. Working with wood on our farm usually meant picking up the remains of a gate or fence that failed to withstand the inattentive tractor-driving habits of a great uncle, hired man, or older brother.

Truth be told, two events dominated our farm woodcraft.

The first was a firewood-making session in some distant pasture after a summer storm toppled a century-old pecan tree. The massive job required my father operating a balky chainsaw, the hired men hand-splitting the pieces with axes, and my brothers and me toting the straight-grained wedges to a wagon for hauling.

The pecan, when seasoned, warmed the home of two hired men, brothers Howard and Jackie, who lived with their mother Clara and younger brother Orlie in a two-story house supplied by the farm.

Howard, the oldest brother, was a maestro of the woodstove; he could make the family's Warm Morning stove radiate heat like the summer sun. A good sense of smell revealed his trick: a shovelful of southern Illinois coal on top of a bed of pecan embers turned the home's parlor into a Florida beach.

Well, okay, a Florida beach where someone was always frying pork.

The remaining trunk of the fallen tree was hauled to a neighboring sawyer who cut it into piles of heavy, five-quarter 2×6s. The nearly indestructible boards were fashioned into fences around the dairy barn.

The farm's other wood-centered event was gathering the remnants of once-working fences, gates, and other implements to heat three butchering kettles each February. That we had enough splintered kindling to keep three kettles bubbling with water, lard, or head cheese for two days was grim testament to our farm crew's destructive ability.

Yet our collective wood skills weren't all destructive; sometimes they were constructive.

For example, in the late-1950s or early '60s, I recall my mother's father, a talented woodworker by trade, helping my father build a 40×60 or so loafing shed for the farm's dry cows. It still stands, strong and square.

We built other farm items from wood, too, like all our hay wagon beds and the boxes of our first silage wagons. In the shade of our maple tree, my father constructed the beds and boxes from various stacks of knotty yellow pine.

Dad's carpentry tools were few. He had only a set of sawbucks, a folding ruler, a hammer, a square, one good handsaw, a nail apron, and an electric circular saw, yet, a couple of days of measuring, sawing, and hammering always yielded a working wagon of some sort.

Good as my father was as a wagon builder, my mother's father was the true craftsman. So talented was he that a farming life gave way to a career in carpentry, then to furniture building, then to pure art. Self-taught, Grandpa spent long, quiet days in his basement shop shaping, sanding, and gluing together tables, chairs, and, on occasion, church lecterns and pulpits.

This small man of great ability, however, died young, and most of what I remember of him and that basement is the earthy mixture of red oak and sweat as he made another dining room chair or rocking chair that my grandmother later upholstered or caned. My mother prizes one of his rockers and still treasures a small box of his favorite hand tools.

I, however, have none of his tools or talent. I do have a piece of furniture he and Grandma collaborated on. Its tight tenons and glowing walnut hold secrets I long to know and likely never will.

It was Halloween, the day I took a solo drive south to visit my parents and, after lunch, to Indian Farm. I took a back way to it, not the usual St. Leo's Road, and I was quickly taken by the emptiness of my old neighborhood: no houses, no barns, no people. If I were to write this column today, I would note that certain grim reality, not uncertain hope.

ONLY THE LAND LASTS FOREVER
NOVEMBER 8, 2009

The final Saturday in October swept me three hours south for lunch with my parents and nearly new grandniece and, later that Halloween afternoon, backwards about forty years for visits with some ghosts on the farm of my youth.

It began as an afternoon drive from my parents' home in town down to the Bottoms, that black gumbo-and-sand plain mostly on the Illinois side of the Mississippi just south of St. Louis. But a peek-a-boo sun pulled me down the limestone bluffs and into the past.

Like most times, the slow descent raised the haunting voices of the Native Americans, French colonists, British soldiers, and American revolutionaries who, over the centuries, laid claim to that land. Upon first seeing it, I reckoned, all must have reveled in their incredible fortune.

This place, I heard them whisper solemnly, is a place of possibilities.

At the base of the bluff I zigged, then zagged through the decaying little village of Modoc. When I was a kid, Modoc had fifty-four residents and equal possibilities. It also had two taverns, one general store, a blacksmith shop, a post office, a gas station, and the home of the county sheriff conveniently next door to the tavern he once owned. As such, the little burg fairly hopped.

Few things, and even fewer of its residents, there hop today. One tavern remains because, it seems, Modoc without a tavern would be like Paris without a tower.

I followed the bluff south past old neighbors' farms but soon had to slow to get my bearings. I was on the right road, yet many of its landmarks had vanished and the ones that still stood were unrecognizable.

The green house that had anchored the Behnken farm was gone. Another mile brought another missing farmhouse. Then another.

The latter wasn't just missing a house; it was missing an entire farm. Fences, barns, bins, cats, everything. All that remained were gravestones of corn and soybeans and they said nothing.

The slow passage to my home farm (which was sold, what, ten years ago already?) brought warm, familiar voices.

The levees that ringed three sides of Indian Farm served several, equally important functions: flood protection in the spring, sledding hills in the winter, fescue pastures for dry cows in the summer, and the best place any season to see the entire farm and, maybe, some part of the future. This photo was taken mid-summer, mid-1960s.

Someone unloading a semi-trailer of corn on the home place brought the sound of my father warning me to stay clear of the tractor PTO that powered an auger moving corn to the top of the biggest, tallest bin, all 5,000 bushels of it, in the Bottoms.

A moment later I heard our longtime hired man, Jackie, reply "Right smart," to Uncle Honey's question of how much corn he and Dad had shelled that day.

"Maybe even a little more," Jackie added without looking up from rolling a cigarette.

A quarter mile farther down the road left me in front of the farm's now-sagging dairy barn, a place so filled with memories and voices it was hard to make sense of 'em all. The clearest voice, though, was that of Howard, Jackie's oldest brother and one of the kindest, most caring people on earth.

"Hey, Allie Boy," he'd say as I entered the milking parlor nearly every evening during the harvest season, "nobody showed up on time, so I started without 'em."

No one showed up because his parlor partner, Dad, was on the combine and Dad's replacement, me, was still on the school bus.

I never liked getting stuck in the dairy barn every harvest evening but, then again, I never minded being stuck anywhere with Howard.

I drove another mile to the road's end and then to the top of the massive Mississippi River levee where I stopped for one last look and listen over the land of my upbringing.

It's as empty as it was a century ago, but its beauty and possibilities remain.

FIFTY YEARS AND NO FORGETTING
NOVEMBER 17, 2013

Like most Americans of the 1955 or so vintage, the lovely Catherine and I will spend time this week recalling our personal whos, whats, whens, and wheres of President John F. Kennedy's murder, funeral, and burial fifty years ago.

It is likely though, we won't talk much about JFK's politics and policy because we were too young to be aware of either. The news of his assassination, however, did mark a beginning of our greater education on government, public policy, and politics. That education continues.

And, yes, I remember exactly where I was and who told me of Kennedy's death that early Friday afternoon in November 1963: I was slurping cold water from a drinking fountain after recess when a fourth-grader, Douglas M., passed by and said, simply, "The President's been shot and killed."

I finished my slurp, looked up and said, like any schoolboy might, "Nah uh."

"Uh huh," Doug insisted, "I ain't lying." He didn't look like he was lying. "Go ask anybody," he said.

I didn't have to.

In the few minutes my classmates and I had been on the playground, the awful news of JFK's assassination had ricocheted off of every hill and mountain in America to finally reach our quiet, small Lutheran school in southern Illinois. When we returned to our desks moments later, our teacher, Mr. Tetting, led us in a prayer for the Kennedy family and our nation.

We then went home and did something we had never, ever done before during the day: we watched television, mostly the owlishly wise-looking Walter Cronkite, for the next three days.

National tragedy or not, certain farm routines continued. Cows were milked, fed, and bedded, corn was picked (no farmer finished harvest by Thanksgiving back then), and church was attended.

The Sunday after the assassination, my family and I were walking the long sidewalk to the back stoop of my grandparents' house for our usual, after-church dinner when my grandmother flung open the screen door to its tiny porch and announced, "Hurry, they just shot him! Shot him on TV!"

Him was Lee Harvey Oswald, they was Jack Ruby, and we ran up the porch steps, through the kitchen, and into the living room to watch the resulting chaos on Grandpa's big black-and-white television. We sat in silence until Grandma said, "It's all just unbelievable. I need to make gravy."

Sometime during that family dinner it was decided that my father's family— parents, sisters, brothers-in-law, aunts, uncles, nieces, and nephews—would all come to our farm the next day, Monday, for a national day of mourning and the day of the Presidential funeral. The plan was to hunt quail and rabbit in the morning and watch the funeral and burial in the afternoon.

And that's exactly what happened.

What didn't happen was work. I had never seen the big farm of my youth, with over 700 acres, 100 milk cows, four hired men, and my father, not work on a workday. This was a first and, in fact, a last.

That day, a sad, respectful silence fell over our farm and nation, comparable only to the deeply sad, awful silence that followed September 11, 2001.

Strange, but I don't remember us eating during the day of President Kennedy's funeral (that, too, would have been a first in the history of German Lutheranism) but I know we must have. I do remember, however, almost every detail of the funeral procession because of the reverent silence the entire, extended family observed during the TV broadcast of it and the burial.

Historians say that television came of age that weekend; it grew from an occasional fancy to a national need because it brought America together to grieve and grow. It did just that, and so did we.

And now we remember because we cannot, and never will, forget.

A "RIGHT SMART" THANKSGIVING
NOVEMBER 22, 1998

Out of the chilly grayness of the mid-November evening, Orlie wobbled toward the back door of our farmhouse. His normal gait, more a lazy stroll than a determined walk, was even more exaggerated by the long-handled loads he appeared to be toting in each hand.

"Missus Reech," he drawled slowly, addressing my mother in the southern Illinois custom of her husband's first name, Rich, "Mr. Reech gave me permission to hunt some of them geese been landin' back on your slough. And, well," Orlie said with a rise in his voice, "tonight I got a right smart bunch of 'em. Can you and Mr. Reech use a couple?"

Orlie raised his arms to bring two plump Canada geese into the evening's fading light. Each was gripped around its elegantly long neck by the man's big, sun-browned hands. Vacant eyes stared out from their jet black faces, but no blood stained their fluffy, chocolate-colored chests.

"Why sure, Orlie," my mother said politely through the partially opened storm door, "and thank you. We'll roast them for Thanksgiving." My brother and I were then sent out to fetch the fat birds.

"Ain't nothing," countered Orlie as he slipped back into the gathering shadows. "I got a right smart bunch and we can't eat 'em all." He then moseyed off.

Off to the "we" he had referred to, his two older bachelor brothers—the farm's principle hired men, Jackie and Howard—and their aging, recluse mother, Clara, tucked in a tenant house a brisk ten-minute walk away; or twenty for the slow-as-molasses Orlie.

"At least they're in season," one of my brothers muttered after the hunter was out of earshot.

It was a commentary on Orlie's habit of shooting game, federal and state law notwithstanding, whenever the doomed prey crossed his gun sights. Year 'round we heard the habitually unemployed man's ever-employed 12-gauge roar and we'd say, "Sounds like Orlie found some ducks." Or rabbits, or quail, or squirrels, or geese, or doves, or deer.

No one griped about Orlie's January 1 through December 31 hunting season. He was simply doing what his family had always done in those wildlife-rich Mississippi River bottoms. If you had enough money for a box of No. 2 Winchesters, you always have the time to put 'em to use. Which, for guys like Orlie was really anytime.

When he wasn't hunting deer or ducks, Orlie usually could be found hunting mushrooms or pecans or ginseng, he called it "shang," or hubcaps or "sodie" and beer bottles for their penny or two-cent deposits.

If and when, as he would say, Orlie accumulated a peach basket–full, a brother would haul him and his "valuables" to Roots Tavern, a couple of miles up the dusty road, to collect his recycling ransom. The money, just a buck or two, was immediately returned to the barkeep for a slim, red tin of Velvet tobacco or a box of No. 2s. Or No. 6s if doves were flying.

One summer Orlie even hunted up enough scrap lumber, tin, and used nails from a collapsing house on the farm to cobble together a fairly respectable dirt floor garage for his fat-finned Pontiac. Since he was rarely flush enough to buy gasoline at twenty-five or thirty cents a gallon from my father, the garage was a good investment of his unencumbered time and under-used car.

And besides, the tin roof made an ideal drying rack for his usually successful summertime shang digging expeditions.

In his prime during the early 1960s, Orlie seemed to be everywhere and nowhere. He could turn up anywhere on that big farm anytime, yet no one ever caught him hunting anything anywhere anytime.

Especially the game warden, who cruised the tall levee along the river a couple of times a week on the lookout for him. Often as not, we'd hear the bark of Orlie's full-choke 12-gauge echo across the broad Bottoms about the time that wide-bottomed warden was halfway into a Stag beer at the tavern.

And now and then a fat goose, a rack of venison, or some squirrels would come calling in Orlie's ham-sized hands. "Got right smart bunch for us," he'd say very slowly as he presented his tribute.

Right smart. It was a common phrase in the Bottoms back then. No one ever explained its precise meaning. But that cold November feast day it meant a gracious meal on our table.

Indeed, as Orlie might say, it was a right smart Thanksgiving.

REMEMBER ORLIE?
NOVEMBER 22, 2009

Longtime readers may recall a Thanksgiving column ten or so years ago that featured our dinner entrée provided by Orlie, the gainfully unemployed brother of our farm's two hired men, Jackie and Howard.

How did we end up with three brothers, all bachelors, living together in a provided house on the farm along with their widowed mother?

I can't recall, but I know my father employed Jackie, the small, leathery middle brother, to work in the fields and, later, brought on his older, stronger brother, Howard, to help with haying jobs. Howard's gentle disposition quickly promoted him from part-time baler to full-time herdsman in the dairy. He stayed there until his death nearly thirty years later.

Orlie, however, was a different matter. Unlike the firecracker Jackie or the quiet giant Howard, Orlie was burdened with an ability to make people uneasy. Part of it was his size; he was a substantial man with well-defined, tanned arms and a barrel chest.

The bigger part, I suspect, was his face. It wasn't so much tanned as stained a reddish brown and usually carried the shadow of a few days' worth of salt-and-pepper whiskers. Even clean-shaven, its round softness was easily overtaken by a knotty complexion that featured pockmarks from what I always guessed to be childhood measles. All conspired to give Orlie a harder, rougher look than he deserved.

He must have known it, too, because you rarely saw him not smiling. He wasn't a jolly or effusive man, so the smile had to be his way of making people give him a second chance after that first, brief chill. It rarely worked, though, and most folks never got close to him, even in public.

Orlie had another burden that no amount of smiling could overcome; back then people referred to it as being "simple." It didn't mean ignorant or illiterate; it meant mentally handicapped, or intellectually challenged.

I don't know if Orlie could read and write. I suspect he could because brother Howard could. Then again, brother Jackie could not.

I do know, however, that he was as good a shade tree mechanic as I ever encountered and, with nothing more than a hammer, a handsaw, a bucket of used nails, and a pencil, Orlie could, and did, build a garage for his rotating stable of tiring Plymouths, Dodges, and Pontiacs.

His chronic unemployment did not mean he didn't work. Sometimes I would spot him somewhere on the farm either going or coming from something like digging ginseng, hunting mushrooms, picking up soda bottles to claim their deposits, or tearing down an old barn to reclaim the lumber and nails for one of his building projects.

Usually, however, you'd see Orlie moseying, he never really walked, to Earl Gene's (another brother) house a couple of miles south and hard by the Mississippi River levee. An afternoon later you'd see him moseying back home with a couple of catfish for his and his brothers' supper.

And, like I noted in that previous column, every now and then he'd show up on our back porch in the evening twilight with a Canada goose or two just in time for Thanksgiving.

I last saw Orlie twenty-five years ago. He was living with Jackie in a three-room, concrete block house two miles north of my father's farm. During a Thanksgiving visit with Jackie, who was then working at a nearby factory, Orlie shambled in from one of his long walks to reach out a big, still-tanned hand and ask, "Remember me?"

Of course I do, Orlie, and I always will.

COOKING MY OWN GOOSE
NOVEMBER 18, 2012

For the first year in five, the lovely Catherine and I will not be driving a cooler with a thawing turkey buried under dozens of chilled adult beverages and a jar of German sauerkraut to Washington, D.C., for Thanksgiving with the sauerkraut-despising, adult beverage-loving heirs.

Instead, we'll be slicing a bird and playing Euchre at my brother's home near St. Louis. It will be a 350-mile day rather than a 2,000-mile week.

Our Thanksgivings are like that though; they bump along in four- or five-year phases rather than glide for decades in one direction.

For example, cows kept us home most Thanksgivings on the southern Illinois dairy farm of my youth. The first real memory I have of any Thanksgiving is when, as previously documented several years ago in this weekly effort, my mother baked two Canada geese, which were donated by our hired man's poacher-brother, Orlie.

Two events made that day memorable. First was the main dish. My mother, someone who could have taught Julia Child a thing or two about great cooking, was flying blind with those geese and none of 'em made a good landing.

The goose was, well, cooked. Let's just say you have shoes with softer leather than the meat those two birds wore that day.

The second event was equally spectacular: it snowed. Snowfall in southern Illinois was common, sure, but never on Thanksgiving and never so beautiful. The flakes were as big as our wide eyes and they danced and drifted to a symphony we could see but not hear. It was unforgettable.

A few years later, when my brothers and I were of sufficient size and age to help Howard the herdsman in the dairy, everyone but the one designated dairy boy left the farm for some aunt or grandmother's in-town feast.

I often volunteered to be the milk martyr because the downside, missing Grandma's chocolate meringue pie, never matched my personal upside: six or seven hours watching football without any big brothers around. I mean, come on.

Thanksgivings during my college years are a bit of a blur.

I do, however, remember one time. It was one of the three Thanksgivings I was a college freshman or sophomore (yep, that's right) that my now life-long college friend Jim C. and I traveled south to my family's farm in his square-rigged prairie schooner.

Okay, it was in his unheated, Eisenhower-era IH pick-up whose top gear got us hurtling down the interstate at, maybe, forty-nine miles an hour. We were two frozen turkeys when we finally made it to the farm.

Returning to Champaign was easy, though; we followed the rust trail the truck had laid down four days earlier.

When the lovely Catherine and I moved into the big, Victorian house in her hometown in 1986, we began a long, lovely run of Thanksgivings at our home. Each seemed to welcome everyone we knew west of Pittsburgh for an annual four-day blowout.

The revelry began in earnest on Wednesday night with a soup supper for guests, grandparents, and college kids who had traveled the farthest. The next day's turkey dinner lasted the entire afternoon and late into the night. The event often brought forty to fifty family members as well as far-flung friends, many of whom camped out on the big house's many cots, couches, beds, and floors for the fish fry my mother and father co-led the following day, Friday, for our neighbors and even more friends.

In truth, the multi-day gathering was the lovely Catherine's Thanksgiving showcase, displaying her matchless ability to entertain and even more amazingly, feed, dozens of hungry Germans and Irish alike.

Since we were just amateur gluttons, though, we reserved Saturday for digestion and goodbyes and then on Sunday, Catherine and I counted the silver.

Just kidding.

This year feels like the beginning of another run of Thanksgivings different than all the others. Whatever is in store, I am very thankful for my family and the memories. And, like every year since 1961, I'm really, really thankful Mom isn't cooking a goose.

Of course, that doesn't mean I won't cook my own.

WINTER

EAT

As with many farms back then, and even today, winter usually began before the harvest was complete on the southern Illinois dairy farm of my youth. Our seemingly never-ending harvest was mostly because every day's long list of work was dictated by the cows. That meant that time spent on non-cow jobs, like the minor details of planting and harvesting, was (if you'll pardon the expression) squeezed in between the 5:00 a.m. and 4:00 p.m. milkings. Yet even after all the grain had been binned, winter still meant cold barns, cold cows, and cold feet. Warmth came through good food, good friends, and good times. But even then every afternoon, of course, someone, usually my father or me or one of my brothers, would have to leave everyone at home to return to a black-and-white world of milk cows, winter's early darkness, and Hoard the Dairyman.

DECEMBERS PAST
DECEMBER 7, 2003

The gray gloom of December has arrived again and so, too, have the memories of a boyhood on a southern Illinois dairy farm. Most of the warm recollections, however, are of cold cows, cold hands, cold feet, and old machinery.

Jackie, the farm's main field hand, dreaded winter. A small, wiry man who wore a perpetual tan from a lifetime spent in the sun, Jackie was a frozen piece of leather from mid-October to Easter.

Each morning at six, Jackie arrived at the dairy barn stiffened by layer upon layer of cotton, wool, and rubber. A half hour of hot coffee and even hotter swearing about the weather might see him shuck his overcoat. A world-class cusser, Jackie spent many winter days in the dairy barn moaning about the cold.

His older brother, Howard, the dairy's herdsman, rarely commented on the cold. Then again, Howard rarely commented on anything. Maybe he thought

When two or more Gueberts gathered, a card game soon followed. Sitting at the farmhouse's kitchen table are my mother (far right), various cousins, aunts, uncles, and me (facing the camera) in an eight-hand Pinochle game, Christmas mid-1980s. This is a classic scene: all eyes look to Uncle Cliff, Dad's brother-in-law, as he undoubtedly asks, "What's trump?"

Jackie complained enough for the both of them. Howard, however, had every right to complain. Winter weather, mixed with the warm wetness of dairying, caused his skin to crack so badly that his fingers often bled. His trusted remedy, rubbing alcohol, only worsened the problem.

We often urged him to use Bag Balm, the cow-tested, dairyman-approved salve for chapped udders, to relieve his hands' soreness. Sometimes he would do so, but invariably, Howard always returned to the alcohol. By January most of his fingers were wrapped in torn strips of cotton rags and electrician's tape. Alas.

The coldest person on that farm, though, had to be my father. Like Howard, Dad spent every morning and evening in the drafty milking parlor and, like Jackie, he spent most days in the frozen fields, too.

Usually, those early December days were spent picking corn. Only once in my twenty years on the farm do I remember seeing the end of harvest by Thanksgiving. The other nineteen saw Dad eating corn dust and snowflakes from the open seat of a ridiculously tiny, by today's giant standards anyway, IH 303 combine.

Dad's next combine, an Oliver, fittingly sported a heated cab. Of course that meant he fried during June's wheat harvest, but it confirmed his only weather-related admonition: "You can always cool off, but it's hard to warm up."

The difference was lost on me; I was always at war with the weather. Winter meant frostbite; summer meant sweat. Spring and fall were just short reprieves from being either too hot or too cold.

Shorts could have cured some of the summer woe, but no self-respecting farmboy back then wore shorts anywhere except to the pond on Sunday afternoons. And, too, Santa could have brought insulated coveralls, but I reckon his wallet was always too thin to outfit us five farmboys warmly.

The week before Santa's arrival usually brought neighbors and friends to our kitchen for catch-up visits over coffee, Christmas cookies, summer sausage, and cheese. If the visits came in the afternoon, most ended with a nip or two before the cold evening milking ensued.

December also meant "doing the books," a yearly paperwork war loathed by the farm's managing bookkeeper, my mother. A card table in the living room signaled the opening battle, but the tiny workspace quickly disappeared under cancelled checks, depreciation schedules, and shortened tempers.

If the fieldwork and paperwork were done and the weather turned snowy, my older brother Rich, my parents, and I often gathered at the kitchen table to play Euchre or 500 during the gray afternoons. The games were as loud and serious as a knife fight, which they often resembled, and gloriously fun.

Despite the cold, the cows, and the complaining, those Decembers were warmed by good food, lasting friendships, a hot card game or two, and more laughter than we had shared all year.

The embers of those December days warm me still.

Just a year and a half into writing the Farm and Food File, I wrote the following column to celebrate Christmas 1994. Aside from the "View from the Levee" column about The Great Flood of '93, this was the first column that ventured away from ag and food policy journalism to meander more towards farm folk and farm memories. Much to my surprise, the Christmas story of Howard, Mary, and Joseph was a smash. I received hundreds of letters from readers and editors saying thanks, sharing their own memories, and asking for more such efforts. (This was when writing a letter meant sitting down with pen, paper, and stamps. These days I still receive plenty of reader mail, but it's mainly the electronic variety. I still keep 'em all though, whether they're written in shaky cursive or Times New Roman, font size 11.)

A Christmas or two following its initial publication, I decided to revive Howard's Christmas column and offered it to my editors to print again if they wanted. All did and an annual tradition began. Now, the week before every Christmas, I send my editors two columns: one based on current reporting of a timely ag policy topic, the other, "Howard's Priceless Gift of Simple Giving." Nine out of ten editors continue to reprint the 1994 column and, still, the responses pour in. Many readers tell me they clip the column to read with their family at holiday gatherings. Others write to say it brings them tears of joy while remembering their own Christmases spent on similarly cold, hardscrabble farms from those long-gone days. I know what it continues to do for me: I still smell the remains of Howard's fried pork supper, still taste the homemade wine, and still marvel at the wondrous "best Christmas ever" Howard and I shared together.

Indeed, the next nineteen years of Indian Farm columns about Honey, Jackie, Orlie, Mrs. Reech, and so many others would have likely never been written, had this piece not been so warmly received.

HOWARD'S PRICELESS GIFT OF SIMPLE GIVING
DECEMBER 25, 1994

The Christmas tree was a scrub cedar hacked from the edge of the woods that bordered our farm. Big-bulbed lights, strung in barber pole fashion, generated almost as much heat as the nearby woodstove. Yellowed Christmas cards, saved over the years and perched like doves on the untrimmed branches, served as ornaments.

"I believe this is the prettiest tree I've ever had," Howard proclaimed as we stood in its glow. "And its smells good, too."

The only scent evident to me was a mixture of wood smoke and the remains of a fried pork supper. But I lied and said, "Sure does."

Howard beckoned me to sit. We had shared this Christmas Day in the dairy barn and it was his request that we share a bit of the night, also. He knew I was alone because my family, his employer, was visiting relatives in town. I knew he was alone because he was always alone, a bachelor for nearly forty years.

"I'll get us some Christmas cheer," he offered as I sank into the sofa. In untied work shoes, he shuffled toward the kitchen. A minute later, he returned with two water glasses filled with rhubarb wine. We raised them to the day.

"It's been a good Christmas, ain't it Allie Boy?" he asked as he sat in a ladder-back chair by the stove.

He had called me Allie Boy for as long as I could remember. I had taken to calling him Hoard the Dairyman, after the title of a farm magazine my father subscribed to.

I nodded. It had been a good day. Two wobbly newborn calves greeted us when we arrived at the dairy barn, sixteen hours earlier. Wet and shivering, we dried them with the past summer's straw before showing them how to find breakfast at their mamas' sides. One was a bull, the other a heifer.

"We ought to name 'em Mary and Joseph," Howard now said as we rehashed the day, "on account of them being born today."

Mary and Joseph? Generally, Howard had only one name for all cows: Succum. None of us knew what it meant or where it came from, but from the time he arrived on the farm in 1965 every cow was always Succum and every calf was always Little Succum. A group of cows or calves were simply Big Succums or Baby Succums.

"Mary and Joseph they will be," I said approvingly.

Silence hung in the stale air. I reckoned that if you had "bached" it for forty years like Howard, silence wasn't a void that always needed to be filled. So I worked on my wine and said nothing. Howard reached for his pipe and the big red can of Velvet that had been my Christmas gift to him that morning.

"You want to roll yourself a smoke, Allie? I got some papers here."

I shook off the offer.

"Yep," Howard said as if to himself, "that's the prettiest tree I've ever had. And this is shaping up to be the best Christmas I've ever had because you came by."

I looked at the tree and then at the old man ringed in tobacco smoke staring at it and I felt sad. Not for him. I felt sad for me. I had agreed to come to his house to accommodate him, a favor for an aging hired man.

But he had not wanted a favor. All he had wanted was the chance to share his Christmas good fortune with me. He had some wine, a warm fire, his prettiest Christmas tree ever, and a week's worth of tobacco. He was happy and he wanted to give me some of that happiness.

As I stared at the silhouette of Hoard the Dairyman in the glow of the Christmas lights, I saw a man of great warmth, vast wealth, and pure honesty. He didn't have a checking account or credit card but he was far richer than the condescending college boy on his sofa.

"Well Hoard," I said a very quiet minute later, "I better go. We both have to be at the barn early tomorrow."

He led me to the back door. "Don't forget," he said as I headed for the truck, "we'll call those calves Mary and Joseph."

Almost forty Christmas Nights later, I have not forgotten the two calves named Mary and Joseph, and Howard's priceless gift of simple giving.

> We Guebert children instinctively knew that Christmas would never bring us wheelbarrows of toys, or unthinkable presents like transistor radios or shiny new Schwinns. We pretty much understood that Christmas would bring one toy in addition to our annual replenishment of flannel pajamas and wool socks. That is, until my older brother David figured out how to stack the deck in his favor. After that incredible awakening, well, let's just say bicycles and radios suddenly came within reach.

THE TRUTH ABOUT SANTA
DECEMBER 16, 2007

Of the many memories I have of Christmas on the southern Illinois dairy farm of my youth, I don't have a single memory of ever telling Santa what I wanted.

I do remember being told innumerable times that I had better be good, or Santa wouldn't bring me what I wanted. How could he, was my internal dialogue, when I hadn't told him what I wanted?

A photograph exists of my older brothers, sister, and me with a department store Santa in, maybe, 1960. Hmm, could I have slipped the fat man a slim list that day?

I doubt it because the picture shows him looking blankly right into the camera while we're all looking at anything but. Eyes don't lie; the disconnect between that St. Louis Santa and those Illinois farm kids couldn't be more obvious.

I do have a clear memory of Santa bringing me a battery-powered, toy electric razor one year. The proof is another photo with me holding the razor while sporting a smile brighter than the tinsel-draped cedar tree behind me.

That razor was way cool, but I didn't ask Santa for it.

A couple of Christmases later my two older brothers received BB guns, the pinnacle of every boy's Christmas gift pyramid. They must have asked Santa for 'em because I had not and, well, what do you think happened?

At that point, anyone with a thinner skull might have picked up on that Ask Santa thing. Me, no. I needed confirmation.

Finally, in 1964 or so, I learned the full truth at Grandma Guebert's house. I remember the precise moment of complete, silencing clarity.

That Christmas Eve was like every Christmas Eve; we were at Grandma's eying the beautifully wrapped gifts under the tree while the adults were in the kitchen eating pickled herring and raw oysters, Grandpa's Christmas gift to them all. Ach, some gift.

As I bored through the tottering pile, I uncovered an enormous box that was ticketed for my brother, David. Wow, David had hit the Grandma jackpot. The Mother Lode.

"David," I said as I pointed in hushed awe, "look!"

"Yeah, I saw that," he said blankly.

"No, dummy," I insisted, "this is the Big One, the . . ."

Before he could slug me into silence, the adults appeared and the great gift giveaway began. I immediately snatched David's package and handed it to him with a command to open it.

Before he had it half unwrapped, I saw what it was.

Oh. My. Goodness. An electric slot car racetrack set.

I fell to my knees, a puddle of quaking disbelief. Looking into that box was like looking into the sun. It was blindingly spectacular, completely incomprehensible.

"I . . . I . . . I can't believe it," I stammered.

"Believe it," David replied coolly. "I already knew I was getting it."

"You peeked under the wrapping?"

"No, I just asked for it."

"What?! You mean you asked Santa?"

"No, stupid. Grandma. She asked me what I wanted Santa to bring and I told her."

"Wait. You told GRANDMA you wanted Santa to bring you a slot car racetrack?"

"Yeah. That's the way it works, idiot."

I looked at the slot car set, then at David, the owner of it *and* a BB gun, then at Grandma.

I had been an idiot. Santa was real and his pipeline was a gray-haired, gravy-making lady named Grandma. I became a true believer right then and there.

And I still believe.

This year, for example, I asked for a bottle of lovely, and purely medicinal, elixir from Scotland's Isle of Skye and a new golf driver from a guy named Callaway. Santa's helper filled the order last Saturday.

All I have to do now is wrap 'em and wait.

The St. Louis department store Santa and Richard, David, Peggy, and me barely holding on in front. This photo is from 1959 or 1960; our younger brothers Perry and Christian literally weren't in the picture yet. Santa knew where the camera was; we farm kids hadn't a clue. My mother sewed our winter wool coats.

OUR BLACK AND WHITE CHRISTMAS
DECEMBER 17, 2000

A white Christmas was a rare event on the southern Illinois dairy farm of my youth. However, with 100 Holsteins to milk twice each day, Christmas always began and always ended black and white.

The day was particularly so for our main milking man, Howard. A life-long bachelor, Hoard the Dairyman, as I called him, worked December 25 as if it were June 25. From 5:00 a.m. until 7:00 p.m., he would do what he did six days a week, fifty-one weeks a year: feed the cows, clean up after the cows, milk the cows.

And if mild weather prevailed on Christmas, Howard did what he did every mild winter's day: he spread manure. Hoard's dedication to this earthly duty never failed to impress my father and depress my mother.

The day before Christmas was different, though. Christmas Eve was the bigger, more celebrated holiday for Hoard the Dairyman and for my family.

Since Hoard always worked Christmas, he was always off Christmas Eve. That meant he'd mosey into the dairy barn around mid-morning December 24 where my father, my older brothers, and I were doing chores. He'd be toting his three perennial holiday gifts: a toothless smile, a box of Brach's chocolate-covered cherries, and an unsealed pint of Jack or Jim. The cherries were for our family; the slug of what Hoard called "Christmas cheer" was for my father.

An hour later, Hoard would usually surrender to the inevitable emptiness of his day and return to his house and its pot-bellied stove to cheer himself into a sloppy stupor.

By the time Hoard was roasted inside and out, the big part of our day was just beginning. Santa always came to our farmhouse Christmas Eve afternoon. Such a clever fellow; he knew to come between milkings. Then my father's parents would arrive from town and, on occasion, so would Uncle Honey and Aunt Esther.

Grandma and Grandpa never brought their gifts for us then; they were saved for that day's second Christmas gathering in their home following the annual Lutheran school Christmas program.

When Uncle Honey and Aunt Esther came, however, they carried one wrapped present apiece for their five grandnephews and single grandniece. It was a grab bag, though, because Aunt Esther never put nametags on gifts. A small package usually meant socks; a large one, pajamas or a flannel shirt.

Honey and Esther took presents to the hired men and their families, too. Once, a hired man came to work after Christmas sporting a gold wristwatch. "Honey gave it to me," he announced; "it sure is perdy." It was also perdy useless because we were perdy sure he couldn't tell time.

After presents, the annual Christmas Eve battle between my mother and her mother-in-law ensued. It always began with the same match: Grandma announcing the younger kids would go to town now with her and Grandpa to avoid the evening milking rush that was "certain to make everyone late" for the school Christmas program. My mother always protested and always lost. Off we'd go to town, my father and older brother Richard to the barn, and my mother to the kitchen.

But Dad, Mom, and Richard always arrived at the school gym on time, thus setting the stage for next year's inevitable battle, to hear 170 children sing and recite every Christmas carol and Christmas Bible passage attributable to Martin Luther and the Missouri Synod. Or so we thought.

Then off to Grandma's house, where the greatest gifts known to kiddom awaited. Grandma was tight with old St. Nick; she always delivered. An annual haul might include sleeping bags, a wool sweater, a baseball mitt, and the perfect gift: a crisp five- or ten-dollar bill.

Later came a buffet meal of icy shrimp, ugly oysters, pickled herring and tongue, olives, saltines, cheese, fancy cookies, and spiked fruitcake. Then, with our bellies full and our dreams fulfilled, home to the farm we went.

Christmas morning I'd rise before five to walk to the dairy barn in the light of the Star of Bethlehem. Upon arrival, I'd be met with a bleary-eyed Hoard and another black and white holiday. It was wonderful.

BOOKS, PLANS, AND CONGRESS
JANUARY 5, 2014

A couple of weeks into every new year, most folks review, often regretfully, their list of resolutions already bent, broken, or buried.

That never happened on the southern Illinois dairy farm of my youth for one simple reason: we never made New Year's resolutions.

In fact, I can't recall a single instance of anyone on that farm (my parents, us six kids, Uncle Honey, Jackie, Howard, Monroe, Bob, Bill, Charlie, Orlie . . .) even mentioning New Year's resolutions let alone making any.

Instead, most of the week between Christmas and New Year's was spent "doing the books." The farm's year-end accounting session was a three-day, number-numbing marathon my parents ran from a folding table in the living room. Likely because it was the warmest, least-used room in the house.

The gear they used never varied: a stack of column-after-column ledger sheets, an ancient adding machine, a raft of pencils, the farm's checkbook, a bottomless pot of coffee, and a grim German resolve to march straight through the endless miles of receipts, cancelled checks, and depreciation schedules until victory—a balanced bottom line—was successfully achieved.

It was a serious job and we children knew it. One clue to its joyless duty was that it was the only time all year we saw our father remain in the farmhouse for three straight days. With a herd of cows to manage and a crew of hired men to boss, the Boss usually only came inside to eat, shave, and sleep. During "the books" he did all three but rarely left.

Another clue was that one of my brothers or I often would be drafted about mid-afternoon to take Dad's place in the dairy barn and share the evening milking with Howard. Evening milkings were otherwise always on Dad's daily schedule, but my determined-to-finish mother kept him inside and tethered to the books, cows or no cows.

The bookwork was necessary for two reasons: taxes and congress with a small "c." Taxes were taxes; you ran the numbers (who knew cows were both taxed and depreciated?) to see what tribute you owed Uncle Sam and the governor. Congress, however, was not Congress on our farm.

Our farm's congress was the annual meeting of the farm's four partners. The partners included my grandfather Victor Guebert, his brother Uncle Honey, and two other, off-farm businessmen. (Note the farm's day-to-day managers, my father and mother, weren't official partners.) These sober number-crunchers met the first or second Saturday every January to review last year's books, consider my father's business plan for the new year, and vote to either adopt, alter, or kill both.

The meeting, held in our home and behind a closed door, was a tense time for my parents because it was a three- or four-hour dissection of one year's work and another year's dreams. Hope usually trumped dread; in fact, I can't recall congress ever disagreeing with any of my father's big initiatives.

And many were big. In the mid-1960s, congress underwrote a complete remodeling of the dairy from a slow, six-cow bypass parlor to a fast, double-six herringbone complete with weigh jars and a new 1,000 gallon stainless steel bulk tank.

A couple of years before that, our farm was the first that I knew to buy what was then called a "self-propelled combine." It was tiny, smaller than today's pick-up trucks, but that baby Massey was an ingenious collection of gears, belts, and augers that somehow threshed wheat and shelled corn while also moving forward.

Also, from the mid-1960s through the mid-1970s, an upright silo was built every other year. First came the 50×24 poured concrete silo. Three stave silos, a 60-footer for the dairy cows, a 40-footer for the heifers and, finally, a 70-footer for the dry cows, followed in quick order.

All were built, as was the entirety of that farm, on careful planning after an annual, days-long slog through the books. The farm's congress, after all, wanted hard numbers and even harder facts, not resolutions.

Sounds like good advice for that other Congress.

SNOW DAY
JANUARY 16, 2011

Two fat sparrows sit in a bird feeder's trough outside my office window as they eat their way through today's snowstorm. Six feet away, a squadron of chickadees performs a touch-eat-and-go dance on a second feeder. In the snow below, a plump dove dines on the sorghum scattered by the unmannered sparrows.

As I sip my coffee and watch this home entertainment center, my thoughts slide back to snowy days on the southern Illinois dairy farm of my youth. While we didn't receive an abundance of snow, winters usually brought at least one day of stay-home-from-school weather. Some years, and a lot of hard praying, brought two or three snow days.

Yes, I confess, as a schoolboy I prayed more for snow in January than a more dedicated farmboy might for rain in July. The reason was simple: you couldn't sled on the fescue-wearing levees that ringed the Bottoms in July, but you could in January if they wore a blanket of snow.

And we did. If the snow was too deep for the school bus to safely slide down the big bluffs that stood guard over our part of the Mississippi River flood plain, it probably was deep enough for my sister, brothers, and me to glide down the levees that guarded the farm from the Mississippi River.

Snow pants? Ski jackets? We weren't on TV; we were on the farm.

A sledding adventure simply warranted wearing two of everything: jeans, socks, flannel shirts, wool hats, and jersey gloves. After piling it all on, off we'd slog the quarter-mile or so to the huge, steep levee. Then we'd launch ourselves downward, reaching astonishing speeds while leaving screams and laughter hanging in the air far above and behind us.

The racecar-like ride had only one drawback: the wide, flat shoulder on which the levee sat was also home to a four-strand, barbed-wire fence. From the top of the levee, that fence—which made our section of levee into a wonderful summer pasture for dry cows—resembled an egg slicer. Halfway down it looked more like a kid slicer.

To avoid the tragedy of an early demise, our trick was to bail off the sled just as the levee's steep slope met the flat shoulder, twenty or so feet before the slicer.

We always nailed the dismount, except one time I froze—either out of fear or nihilism, I can't remember—and remained glued, belly down, on the sled. My brothers yelled, my sister screamed, and I flew, unthinking and unsliced, under that fence.

My brother David dove under the wire and ran to me, eyes the size of milk buckets.

"It's a miracle!" he shouted. "How'd you do it?"

I don't know, but I do know no one ever tried it again. Miracles, we suspected, were like lightning bolts; they don't strike the same place twice.

Several years later, when brother Rich and I were both on the farm after college, snowy afternoons brought card games with our parents. Rich and I partnered against Mom and Dad in red-hot games of Pinochle, Euchre, or 500. We'd play until the light faded and the cows came home.

And when they did, Rich or Dad or I would join the ever-faithful Howard in the dairy barn for the evening milking.

Now, as daylight fades on another snowy day decades later, I'm pretty sure my two older brothers, one at work in Sparta, IL, and the other driving to a meeting in northern Georgia, looked out pensively on the newly fallen snow where they were. One likely wondered how I had survived the barbed-wire slicer; the other got an itch to play Euchre or 500.

I know I did.

Winter butchering was a fat time to be on the dairy farm of my youth. It was an all-hands-on-deck and all-knives-and-forks-welcome convergence of neighbors, storytelling, and farm-raised food. As a kid, I often thought butcherin' days were the farm's best days of the entire year. I still think that because I can't remember any other time of the year everyone worked as closely. Putting up eight or ten hogs from snort to sausage in a few days was real work, and more happily done and more neighborly shared than the rest of our annual workload. I dearly miss that camaraderie, that delicious reward, that sense of shared purpose.

BUTCHERIN' WEATHER
FEBRUARY 5, 2006

If the weather forecast for the southern Illinois dairy farm of my youth promised three or four cold and clear days in early February, the work forecast promised three or four days of hot and heavy hog butchering.

The exciting event, at least for my brothers and me, began with a bloodless day of ritual preparation.

The tip-off arrived with Jackie, the farm's main field hand, loading scrap lumber on a hayrack. Old fence posts, broken gates, and busted barn boards would be fuel to heat the three, soot-caked kettles needed for the coming days' work.

Jackie and my father would then tote the enormous cast iron kettles from the back of the machine shed and place each on tri-cornered stands in the center of the farmlot.

Next, six or eight carcass-holding single trees were hung in the east-facing bays of the machine shed, and rough-cut oak butchering tables, glistening from years of raw pork fat rubbed into their tops, were brought from a nearby smokehouse.

Enormous knives with shiny, freshly-honed edges and a couple of meat saws were placed like surgeon's instruments on another, smaller table. So too were a borrowed electric sausage grinder and the farm's gallon-and-a-half, hand-cranked sausage stuffer.

Late that day, a hog-producing neighbor would bring the event's main characters. Color or breed mattered little to my father; he liked all long and rangy sows equally.

"More pork chops and more lard in those older gals," he'd explain each year. A temporary pen in the machine shed held them until dawn and their demise.

Since every employee's annual pay included a hog—two if, like my father, he was married with children—butchering on our farm usually meant slicing, dicing, and rendering six or eight, and some years, ten hogs.

In turn, that meant the first actual day of butchering was a long day of killing, scalding, scraping, gutting, and splitting hog after hog. We also saved much of the blood to make blood sausage late that first afternoon.

That night's supper was, without fail, fried pork brains. And, yes, they were as awful as they sound. We kids choked them down in hateful silence.

I broke the silence, however, as a teenager when I bit down on a cracker-and-egg battered brain patty and, you guessed it, nearly cracked a tooth on a flattened .22 caliber slug. It was the last meal of brains and bullets I ever attempted to consume.

The really big butchering day was the day thereafter when the chilled carcasses, hung overnight in the open air, were broken into primals, then sliced into cuts.

Before that act, however, organ meat, jowls, and other unsavory slabs went into one kettle to make a meaty porridge we called liver sausage. When cooled, though, its high fat content held it together like concrete. A second kettle slowly stewed buckets of belly and back fat into lard.

Uncle Honey took charge of both. The lard-rendering fire had to be hot enough to "crack" the fat into lard and cracklings, but not too hot to burn or

End of day one of hog butcherin', sometime in the early-1960s. Day two brought lard to render, head cheese to cook, sausage to grind and stuff, and freezers to fill. If you were a kid on the farm, there was no grander place to be than with the men as they killed, cut, and cussed hogs in February.

embitter the lard. Honey stirred and stoked the lard and liver sausage into soupy perfection.

In the meantime, the hired men and my father hand cut and divvied-up all the chops, roasts, and steaks, trimmed the bacons and hams, and began grinding raw pork into sausage.

My mother, of course, was everywhere. She made certain the sausage was seasoned just right, dictated how the meat was to be cut, always kept an eye on Honey so he didn't burn the lard to a crisp or the farm to the ground, prepared the sausage casings, and, in her spare time, cooked and served every meal.

The most special meal was supper that meat-making day: the freshest pork sausage possible, mashed potatoes, and sauerkraut.

Afterwards, washtubs of chops, roasts, and sausage were brought to the dimly-lit basement where an assembly line of wrappers, tapers, markers, and haulers soon delivered the meat to one of our two deep freezers.

Then, until the following February again brought good butcherin' weather, we lived high off the hog of our hard labor.

A TALE OF TWO ECONOMISTS
FEBRUARY 24, 2008

Everything I know about economics is shaded by the guiding philosophies of my two earliest teachers on the topic. The first was Jackie, our farm's longtime hired man; the second was my first econ professor at the Big U. One was yin; the other yang.

"Economics," the professor solemnly pronounced that first day of class in 1973, "is neither art nor science. It is, instead, the near-perfect marriage of art and science."

The art part, as I came to learn later, was taught by the College of Business; the science part by the College of Agriculture. The tweedy biz boys spent entire semesters lecturing about guns and butter while the pocket-protected aggies spent every class demanding hard numbers—demand elasticities, points of diminishing returns, variable costs per acre.

That hard-soft/science-art difference seems to persist today.

The U.S. ag economy, fueled by rock-hard global supply and demand, continues its rocket ride to beyond the stars. On February 12, the U.S. Department of Agriculture estimated 2008 net farm income would top $92 billion, a four percent bump above 2007's all-time record and a shattering fifty-one percent above the rolling, ten-year average of $61 billion.

At the same time, however, you can't swing a soybean-inked *Wall Street Journal* without smearing your fingers with evidence that last summer's mortgage fever continues to sicken the general economy: rising unemployment; tepid job growth; falling housing values; Wall Street selling arms, legs, and backsides to any sailor with cash in his pocket.

To this former student of Econ 101 and 102 and Ag Econ 100, 220, 232, 324, 325, and 340, these conflicting facts might be better explained by hired man Jackie's sole insight to macro, micro, and ag economics: "It's these (mild expletive) Republican times."

Jackie didn't mean the Richard Nixon Republican times we shared back then. Rather, he meant his childhood, belly-to-the-backbone days of "that (really explicit expletive) Herbert Hoover" and the Depression. Jackie never forgot being hungry and never forgave Hoover.

Indeed, any time gas prices nosed up a nickel or the price of a pair of bib overalls climbed two bits back then, "Republican times" was the simple, single cause of the outrage he called "enflation."

And Jackie never put too fine a point on any price movement. A tick up or down for corn or wheat or butter or shotgun shells or health insurance, which he called "Blue Cross/White Shield" because of the prominent emblem on the return address of his monthly bill, was "enflation."

If Jackie were alive today, I'm pretty sure today's confounding economic news would kill him. Well, at least perplex him to the point where he'd lean against a barn wall, roll a smoke, and with either me or one of my brothers, "try to noodle it out."

The search, however, would end with his same amen, "Republican times."

While Jackie had no formal schooling past the second grade, he wasn't stupid. Nor, as I was to learn, was his colorful explanation of general price activity.

Twenty or so years later, I put Jackie's single economic theorem to the test during an interview with noted Harvard economist John Kenneth Galbraith, a fiercely partisan Democrat. "What," I asked, "will be the result of President Ronald Reagan's massive tax cuts and massive deficit spending?"

"Rack and ruin," announced Galbraith; "which," he added after a pause, "are my nicknames for this Administration's two heroes, Coolidge and Hoover."

"Ah," I suggested, "Republican times?"

"One can say that," he replied.

Someone always did.

IT'S A RIGHT SMART MISS TREE
MARCH 4, 2012

For over twenty years, Jackie served as the main field hand on the southern Illinois dairy farm of my youth. He was a tough piece of sunbaked leather who never weighed more than 150 lbs. when fully clothed, soaking wet, and carrying a ten-pound sledgehammer.

He possessed a hired man's respect for speech; he talked only when talked to and then, most times, only in a collection of southern Illinois' phrases that carried more code than context.

Once my father asked him how much plowing he had completed in a field's far flank. Jackie's reply was a perfectly vague, "Right smart."

My father, not knowing what "right smart" meant, drove to the field to discover the forty-acre field was nearly half plowed. That knowledge, however, raised another question: Was "right smart" about twenty acres or generally about halfway?

That head-shaker had another perfectly vague, often-used Jackie-ism: It's a mystery. The sentence was usually delivered with a noticeable cock of his head to the right and with the operative word sounding more like a two-syllable proper noun, Miss Tree, than a three-syllable common noun, mystery.

Two more things you won't know about Jackie unless I share them: he was illiterate and his given name was Herbert. He could sign his legal name in a slow, shaky hand but he couldn't read any sentence it might appear in.

Jackie comes to mind, as he might to longtime readers who may recall mentions of him throughout the years, more and more as a warm winter and hot political season bring a right smart amount of vapor lock to more brains than usual.

For example, commodity groups, farm organizations, several state legislatures, and many in the ag press are all aflutter over what they breathlessly warn is a well-oiled, vegetarian conspiracy to kill animal agriculture.

Moreover, these worried carnivores—whose livestock are, interestingly, mostly vegan—brook no compromise by any market-driven customer like McDonald's and Chipotle whose diners say they would happily enjoy eggs and bacon from hens and hogs they believe are, well, happy.

What makes a hen or hog happy? It's a Miss Tree, but I reckon it's a very safe bet, or an even right smart bet, that the sixty-seven square inches that compose a caged laying hen's entire world doesn't hold a lot of laughs.

In fact, doubling that space to 124 square inches, or about one-half the front page of the newspaper in your hands, probably doesn't harbor a whole lot more, but it has to hold twice as many of something that goes by the grim name "battery cage."

At least that's what the United Egg Producers (UEP), a nationwide farm cooperative that represents the owners of ninety-five percent of the laying hens in America, believes. UEP is working with the Humane Society of the U.S. to codify federal regulations that its customers know they want for chickens.

And how do these customers, most of whom have never met a chicken, let alone a happy chicken, know? They know by where and how they spend their money; they are customers and they are always right.

Some in the Bacon Gang are getting smarter, too. McDonald's announced in mid-February it would not purchase bacon from any producer that "confines pregnant sows in gestation crates."

Big Mac is a latecomer on the happy hog train. Already on it are Burger King, Winn-Dixie, and Wendy's. Smithfield, the biggest bacon maker in the world, has pledged to hop on by 2017 when all its gestation crates will be gone.

Are these global food sellers anti-meat vegans or are they simply smart marketers who know their customers are always right?

My bet is they're right smart marketers. Smarter, anyway, than anyone who insists they are right and their customers are wrong.

RENEWABLE ENERGY
MARCH 2, 2014

The tall, mostly dead red oak on the eastern edge of the farmette still stands during this late, long winter, saved mostly by this late, long winter.

The majestic, strong-armed tree, my age or a little more, had a date with the saw and maul as soon as the weather turned cold. Deep snow and face-cracking cold, however, kept the aging sawyer close to the woodstove where that oak would, sooner or later, meet its ashy end.

It's not the only dead tree to survive the winter. Most years the wood I saw and split comes from a dozen or so dead trees in a rolling, beautiful hardwood forest owned by a generous farming neighbor. He likes his woods clean; I just like his wood. It's the basis for a years-long deal that keeps him cool and me hot.

This year, however, I've cut nary a cord, jag, or wheelbarrow of anything because while I love to saw, split, carry, and stack wood in the winter cold, I hate doing any of those warm jobs in snow. I like my woodcutting weather like my friend M.A. says he enjoys his martinis: ice cold and very dry.

And neither of us, it seems, likes to get wet anymore.

It was the same on the southern Illinois dairy farm of my youth where a round, tall Warm Morning woodstove glowed hot throughout the winter months in our farmhouse kitchen. Wood for it came from the storm-wracked trees cut, split, and stacked long before any snow fell.

That wood, mostly iron-hard pecan, burned hot as coal. If pecan wasn't handy, sulfur-packed southern Illinois coal was indeed added to the stove to boost its BTUs. I can still smell that coal and still see it aglow in the bottom of that Warm Morning.

Our farm's hired hand bachelor brothers burned wood and coal every day of every winter throughout their decades-long employment. While we often shared the wood from any downed tree with them, they burned far more coal in their two-story, uninsulated tenant house than we.

I recall one evening milking session with Howard, our dairy's herdsman, as he complained loud, long, and uncharacteristically that the price of coal, at about $8 a ton, was "gettin' him hot enough not to need none."

When he cooled off the following week, a big, black pile of eons-old carbon bloomed next to a bare hollyhock near his kitchen door.

Sometime in the early 1960s, central heating was installed in both our home and the milking parlor. I'm not sure how the cows came to be on par with us when it came to indoor heat, but I'm pretty sure the furnace in the dairy barn was bigger, ran better, and supplied more heat than the furnace in our house.

After that upgrade, from a tiny propane heater at one end of the long milking parlor and another, even smaller heater in the bulk tank room, it was easy to find any hired man at any time during any winter day. The cows had their loafing shed; so did the loafers who looked after 'em.

For decades thereafter I cut no wood because the houses the lovely Catherine and I, and later, Paul and Gracie, lived in had no stoves. Then, with Paul and Gracie fledged and flown, we empty-nesters moved to a smaller nest with two woodstoves.

Bone-deep, almost-free wood heat soon followed.

This past fall, both stoves were replaced with smaller, more efficient units. Neither gets fat on the meals of well-seasoned wild cherry, red oak, black walnut, and elm, and each pours forth warmth and delight, no matter its diet.

I'd tell you more but I've got a red oak to take down and split.

Well, sometime.

EPILOGUE

MARY GRACE FOXWELL

While we're on the subject of memories worth preserving, I'd be grateful to share a few of mine. Not of me, but of this book's author.

After several years of working as a staff editor and freelance writer for various magazines, Dad challenged himself to begin writing a weekly column, The Farm and Food File, because he saw a gaping hole in traditional newspaper journalism. No other nationally syndicated columnist focused on the nexus of food, farming, farm policy, and politics; rather, popular columnists at the time tended to focus on just one of these (often polarizing) issues. Long before the slow-food movement took to Facebook and urban foodies flocked to Twitter, Dad recognized the complex convergence of farm and food issues, and in 1993, he decided he was up the challenge of reporting on them. And while I may not have grasped the broad scope of his ambitious mission at the time, I certainly gathered that my father had an unusual job.

Unlike fathers of my friends, neighbors, and classmates, Dad worked from home. His office was a 500 sq. ft., smoke-filled room above an old carriage house that was located roughly fifty feet from our back door. Although his workplace was just a few steps from our kitchen, Dad would often say "Alright then, I'm heading out to the office! Big day!" on his way out, as if he thought we weren't going to see him in exactly nine seconds pick up the newspaper from our driveway and chat with our neighbor Jerry. Paul and I would then roll our eyes as we sleepily ate our cereal.

Dad's job, and general daily routine, seemed odd in other ways, too. He would curiously write the word "self" on my school medical forms when prompted to list his employer. When he wasn't working "up in the office," as we always referred to it, he was tirelessly working on our early 1900s home—climbing scaffolding to paint the out-of-reach eaves, trimming the decades-old yew bushes, and mowing our yard as well as our elderly neighbors' yards—which all seemed to bring him great satisfaction. In fact, Paul and I believed (well, still believe) that Dad uniquely reveled in hard work. On early weekend mornings when most parents would still sluggishly be drinking coffee, we'd find him weeding the driveway, sweeping and scrubbing the front porch, or repainting 1970s patio furniture in the backyard.

His professional attire was also peculiar compared to other dads I knew. While my friends' fathers often wore khakis and button-up dress shirts, Dad's wardrobe consisted mainly of Farm & Fleet statement pieces: weathered carpenter jeans, flannel shirts with patched elbows, a raggedy, tufted Case IH vest, and lace-up, brown leather boots that I referred to as his "Indiana Jones shoes" because the famous archeologist once stopped a runaway mining cart with his feet—while wearing Dad's exact boots! It was a remarkable coincidence that I was sure no other father had experienced.

Dad's daily uniform varied only on Tuesdays and Saturdays. On Tuesday night—his favorite night of the week—Dad would change after supper into a short-sleeved, cotton polo shirt with the name Alan stitched on the front. This beloved bowling league uniform remained unchanged for more than a decade. On Saturdays, he would don a hideous pair of dark green, paint-spattered, canvas coveralls to, I suppose, carefully protect the fraying Case IH vest while he worked in the yard or garage.

He paired the coveralls with an equally paint-spattered Cardinals baseball hat and a radio headset that dated back to the Nixon administration. My friends would often witness this embarrassing ensemble, at which point I would usher them into the house to avoid the worst dressed dad on the block. (Farm and Food File readers may also recall a column in which Dad, while visiting me and my husband Andrew in Washington D.C., was approached by a local resident who kindly offered him a free sandwich. This generous philanthropist had apparently taken one look at Dad and assumed he was homeless.)

Dad's office staff was also a unique and unrivaled bunch. His only co-workers included Mom—the lovely Catherine—and our loyal, lovable mutt Poogie. Poogie leapt into the great doggie unknown in 2000 and was soon replaced by a just-as-lovable, yellow lab Maggie, who, until recently when she also leapt on

Dad's uniform, at the kitchen table of our Delavan, IL, home sometime in the late 1980s. My brother and I still joke that Dad put on the red vest, a much-beloved Christmas gift from his IH-loving in-laws, the first of every October and wore it through June. Dad claims he'd take it off one or two nights to sleep.

after fourteen years, was Dad's steadfast office assistant and the farmette's only livestock besides the well-fed birds.

Given Dad's other, previously noted pursuits, Mom often worked more on the column than he did. For several years, Mom put her career on hold and was Dad's editor-in-chief, bookkeeper, and marketing director. She spent the majority of her day on the phone, convincing newspapers across the country to print and pay for the column. She was, first and foremost, still Mom though—she would call editors, track the outstanding bills, and manage syndication mailings—while schlepping us to and from after-school activities, making homemade strawberry jam, helping us with our homework, and graciously hosting friends and family members several times a week for last-minute dinners or casual get-togethers.

Also of note, since starting the column, Dad's work schedule has remained as predictable as the Knights of Columbus Hall's Friday night menu. His day begins early with coffee and a cover-to-cover read of the local daily newspaper followed by *The New York Times* on his iPad. He researches and works on the week's column from 7:30 a.m. to 12:15 p.m., then breaks for lunch while catching the midday broadcast of *Charlie Rose*. At 1:00 p.m., he retires to his armchair for his afternoon reading of *The Wall Street Journal* and a seventeen-minute nap. (Naps extend longer only on Sunday afternoons, during televised golf tournaments or induced by mowing or gardening fatigue.)

By 2:00 p.m., Dad is back at his desk, where he remains "until the work gets done." Quitting time typically falls between 5:00 and 6:00 p.m. At this point, Dad turns off his computer, turns on NPR's *All Things Considered*, and promptly enjoys a cold Guinness, or three. After dinner at home or uptown with friends, Mom usually heads to bed no later than 9:00 p.m., but Dad stays up reading late into the night. Works by John McPhee, Wendell Berry, David McCullough, and towering stacks of *The New Yorker* are reliably by his bedside.

And after many years of columns, editors, and dark, dark beer, Dad's still at it.

Hmm, sounds like the daily chores, work uniform, and schedule of a humble and loyal hired man I've heard about. The naps, however, sound a lot like a beloved great uncle . . .

I hold other memories, too. In truth, the southern Illinois dairy farm of *my* youth stands in stark contrast to that of my father's. Whereas his memories relate the hard work required to keep up with the fields, garden, dairy, and farmhouse, my childhood memories of Indian Farm evoke only one sentiment: fun-filled adventure.

Mamo and Popo's farm was an expansive kingdom—a seemingly limitless acreage of black earth, machinery sheds, dusty dairy barns, empty silos to peer up in wonderment of, and steep levees from which we could survey our empire. Indeed, by the late 1980s, my grandparents had retired, rented out the farm ground, and we thought, given the farmhouse and surrounding buildings over to their grandkids as the biggest playground we'd ever seen.

Each trip to Indian Farm meant a few, precious days of long-awaited freedom. (It also meant acquiring important life skills, like learning how to shoot Pepsi cans with a BB gun, or, just as important, learning how to properly scrub underneath your fingernails with Lava soap.) My brother Paul and I loved and yearned for those farm visits. A weekend for Easter, a full week in the summer, a long weekend in the fall, and a few days over Christmas were mini-vacations to another world and another life.

We would speed down Lock and Dam Road on ATVs (no helmets required), hunt for arrowheads in the fields with Popo, camp in the fifth-wheel RV parked in the backyard, learn how to bake peach pie and cobbler with Mamo, and run in the ditches with the farm dogs until our grandparents hollered at us to come in for supper.

Supper equated to a cast iron, cauldron-like fryer of fish, a mountain of buttery mashed potatoes, a pan of dinner rolls, and always tall glasses of rich, whole milk. (Okay, there was that one time we had salted pork backbone and I immediately considered becoming an eight-year-old vegetarian.)

If we were still hungry after supper, our grandparents let us snack on whatever else we desired. We'd gulp down chocolate malt milkshakes, stove-popped popcorn, and cake Mamo called "Texas cake" because, I assumed, it had to be the size of that big southern state. We'd fall into bed well fed, extra tired, and very happy.

The next morning meant cinnamon rolls, peanut butter coffee cake, bacon, more milk, and more adventures. Paul and I would spend the morning treasure hunting in the abandoned barns or around the silos, then often go shopping with Mamo in town. That trip scored us new shoes, comic books, Barbie clothes, and any chocolate-coated, extra-sugary cereal we asked for. (My grandmother remains a generous gift-giver to me, Paul, and our cousins. My most recent gifts include a seven-quart, cast iron Le Creuset Dutch oven and a "pretty darn good" boning knife.)

Lunch was Velveeta macaroni, chocolate milk, and Schwan's push-pops. After Popo's post-lunch nap, we'd hop in his truck and drive the levees as he gauged the Kaskaskia. Supper might be hamburgers at a nearby tavern with Mamo and Popo's friends Eddie and Pearl. A rarely enforced bedtime meant that we'd stay up late playing games of air hockey, jumping back and forth between the beds in the big bedroom upstairs, and rolling around on Mamo and Popo's waterbed while they watched the news in the den.

The farm was the best sleep-away camp we knew; we always begged not to leave.

Following big holiday gatherings on the farm, Dad and his brothers would often stay up late playing Euchre at Mamo and Popo's kitchen table. I loved to sit quietly in my pajamas on a stool next to Dad, watching their raucous games and listening to them swap childhood memories.

Listening in on their tales, however, I silently observed that their childhoods were very, very different than mine. Aside from Mamo's unchanged supper menu and the farm's main beverage, it seemed like another farm entirely. Also, cards in-hand and eyes intently focused on the game, they seemed completely unaware that while sharing their individual memories, they all kept repeating the same word again and again.

Work.

Their stories grew louder as they remembered waking up to milk cows before dawn, then walking alone down Lock and Dam Road holding nothing but a flashlight, coming home from school and promptly having to weed the never-tamed garden, helping deliver and "bed" calves in the cold winter, canning fruits and vegetables in Mamo's stifling summer kitchen, and working with Popo in the fields year-round. They also spoke about Mamo sewing all of their clothes—everything from corduroy blazers to cotton underwear—and Popo waking up as early as 4:00 a.m. to start his day.

Remarkably though, they didn't seem disheartened by, in my young opinion, such an utterly un-fun, bleak existence. In fact, they laughed and smiled while recounting all of it.

Now, my brother and I were by no means spoiled city kids; we weren't ignorant of what was required of farm life. We grew up in a small, rural town and many of our friends were farm kids. We also had weekly chores; dusting, vacuuming, watering Mom's flowerbeds, or helping Dad trim the bushes pretty much summed up our not-so-bad list though.

Observing the late-night Euchre games, I realized that the "work" I knew paled in comparison to the Guebert kids' duties of the 1960s and early '70s. To put it simply, our work didn't involve pitchforks, cultivators, balers, or augers. Our summer days were not spent primarily with older hired men, a hay crew, or an accident-prone uncle, either. Paul and I went to movies with our friends, rode bikes with our parents, swam on a local swim team, and performed in community theater productions.

Most notably, and seemingly contrary to the older generation's experiences, every time Paul and I came to Indian Farm, we had nothing but fun, and heard nothing of work.

It was through those early trips to the farm, hearing my family's stories, and later, closely reading Dad's columns, that I gradually came to realize a glaring, almost obvious contradiction: How could a life so hard be remembered so fondly? How could the Indian Farm of Dad's youth, full of back-breaking labor and hours toiling under the hot sun, be the same Indian Farm that I found so magical?

Unlike Christmases on the farm of Dad's youth, I don't think the answer is purely black and white. Instead, it's a fuzzy gray, both simple and difficult to explain.

I did not grow up on a southern Illinois dairy farm, and I did not spend the majority of my childhood and young adulthood working toward a collective family purpose, such as a year-end harvest or a winter butchering session. I did, however, grow up with a wonderful storyteller for a father. And as a young girl, his stories made me realize that he had a profoundly different upbringing than

October 1993. Father and daughter on the front porch of the Big House in town, our home for twenty years until Mom and Dad moved to the nearby farmette in 2005. We made a great team, even back then. He's doing what he did every autumn for more than two decades: scraping, painting, and sweating. I'm doing what I've done since birth: listening dutifully while also loudly reminding my father not to kill himself. (Once, years later when I failed to remind him, he fell from the same porch roof, cracking three ribs.)

I did, but I also realized that he still learned important lessons, still creatively found ways to have fun, and still created warm, lasting family memories.

I am, however, still quite sure that some of his memories of the farm are not so warm, and not so happily recollected.

After much thought and many, long conversations, I've come to the conclusion that Dad's fifteen or so years of Sunday school provided him with plenty of German Lutheran brimstone, for this life and the next, so I believe he made the decision to focus the bulk of his story-telling energies on the memories of people and events that unfailingly brought, and still bring him, enjoyment and pride, instead of on the memories that brought, and may still bring, sadness and regret.

Ever the journalist, Dad reported the hard, indisputable facts (children working adult jobs such as milking 100 dairy cows twice-daily, hauling 90 lb. sacks of soybean meal, canning 100 quarts of peaches, and experiencing serious, farm-related injuries) while also recounting those truths the way *he* remembers them, and the way *he* would prefer them to be remembered. That is, indeed, the beauty of memoir writing: it is a multi-faceted personal, literary, and historical journey. No one can dispute it, but many can relate to and learn from it.

I believe that's exactly why, for more than twenty years, Farm and Food File readers have requested a collection of these Indian Farm stories. Every one of those faithful readers had a Honey, Howard, or Jackie shape and influence their lives at some point, and perhaps some of those readers also have memories of similarly not-so-easy upbringings that they've now come to understand more fully.

Maybe some of you can also personally relate to that situation. Or, if you're like me, you once searched for much clearer answers on how something both is and isn't, but instead now you simply seek the calm and surprising clarity that comes from not having all the answers, not always knowing how or why. And perhaps like me you've also learned that like life itself, a memoir can be, and often is, contradictory.

When I encouraged Dad to consider that these columns could be woven together to form a uniquely personal, but also a profoundly powerful account of life on an American farm, he was doubtful. But when I earnestly asked him to join me in what I knew would be a deeply meaningful project for both of us, in addition to countless others, he agreed. Most likely because, early on, he learned to prefer more work to less work.

I, however, learned early on that love can't be measured in silage bins, wagonloads, or quart jars.

Someone taught me that if you work very hard, love can be measured in words.

ALAN GUEBERT graduated from the University of Illinois in 1980 and has written the nationally syndicated column The Farm and Food File since 1993. His awards include Writer of the Year and Master Writer from the American Agricultural Editors' Association. Alan and his wife, the lovely Catherine, live in rural Delavan, Illinois. He may be reached at www.farmandfoodfile.com.

MARY GRACE FOXWELL graduated from Saint Mary's College in 2007. She and her husband co-direct the social media advisory firm Foxwell Digital in Madison, Wisconsin. Gracie may be reached at www.foxwelldigital.com.

The University of Illinois Press
is a founding member of the
Association of American University Presses.

Designed by Jennifer S. Holzner
Composed in 11/14 Adobe Garamond
with ChunkFive, Gravity, League Gothic,
and Lulo display
by Jim Proefrock
at the University of Illinois Press
Manufactured by Cushing-Malloy, Inc.

University of Illinois Press
1325 South Oak Street
Champaign, IL 61820-6903
www.press.uillinois.edu